District Library Administration

A Big Picture Approach

Cynthia Anderson

Your Trusted
Library-to-Classroom Connection.
Books, Magazines, and Online.

Library of Congress Cataloging-in-Publication Data

Anderson, Cynthia, 1945-
　District library media administration : a big picture approach / Cynthia Anderson.
　　p. cm.
Includes bibliographical references and index.
ISBN 1-58683-154-2 (pbk.)
　1. School libraries—United States—Administration. 2. Instructional materials centers—United States—Administration. I. Title.
Z675.S3A66 2005
025.1'978'0973—dc22

2004019394

Published by Linworth Publishing, Inc.
480 East Wilson Bridge Road, Suite L
Worthington, Ohio 43085

Copyright © 2005 by Linworth Publishing, Inc.

All rights reserved. Purchasing this book entitles a librarian to reproduce activity sheets for use in the library within a school or entitles a teacher to reproduce activity sheets for single classroom use within a school. Other portions of the book (up to 15 pages) may be copied for staff development purposes within a single school. Standard citation information should appear on each page. The reproduction of any part of this book for an entire school or school system or for commercial use is strictly prohibited. No part of this book may be electronically reproduced, transmitted, or recorded without written permission from the publisher.

ISBN: 1-58683-154-2

5 4 3 2 1

Table of Contents

Dedication	vi
List of Copyright Permissions Needed	vi
Acknowledgements	vi
Author Information	vi
Appendices	vii
Table of Figures	viii
Introduction	1
Chapter One: Staffing and Personnel	3
Recruitment and Screening	3
Job Descriptions	7
Interviewing	8
Negotiated Agreements	9
System Staffing Guidelines	9
Staff Evaluation	10
Certification and Licensure Credentials	10
New Staff Orientation and Mentoring Programs	11
Procedures Manual	12
Assisting Building Principals	12
Working with Other Administrators	13
Chapter Two: Policies and Plans	15
Identifying Necessary Policies	16
Developing Effective Policies	19
Policy Development Process	19
Developing a Handbook for Librarians	20
Strategic Planning	25
Tactical Planning	29
Chapter Three: The Collection	31
Selection Policy	31
Collection Development	32
Ordering, Purchasing Methods, and Cataloging	36
Processing Materials	37
Weeding	38
District Role for Inventorying the Collection	42

Chapter Four: Budgets and Funding	45
Operations Budget	45
Capital Budget	47
Fundraising Initiatives	48
Local Foundations	50
Fines	50
Grants	50
Chapter Five: Facilities	55
Maintaining Existing Facilities	55
Planning for New or Renovated Libraries	57
Beginning to Plan	58
Areas to Include in the New or Renovated Library	64
Moving, Relocating, and Closing Libraries	69
Planning to Avoid Disasters	73
Chapter Six: Programming	75
System-Wide Class Scheduling System	75
Curriculum Design	77
Assessment Methods for Library Skills	78
Special Programming	82
Program Evaluation	84
Chapter Seven: Technology	85
Long-Range Library Technology Plan	85
Internet Access	87
E-Rate	87
Internet Filtering and *CIPA*	88
Technology Standards	89
Library Security Systems	89
Video Streaming and Digital Video	90
Instructional Media	90
Instructional Television Programming	90
Instructional Television Production	90
Digital Divide	91

Chapter Eight: Professional Growth and Development 93
    Long-Range Professional Development Plan 93
    Professional Development Committee 94
    Conducting Staff Development Needs Assessment 94
    Results-Based Staff Development 94
    Planning Staff Development 96
    Professional Development Committee 98
    Other Library Media Committees 98
    Opportunities 98
    Evaluation of Staff Development Sessions 99
    School Improvement Initiatives 99
    The Director's Professional Development and Growth 100
    Credentials 100
    Leadership 100

Chapter Nine: Advocacy 103
    Advocating for People 103
    Getting Positive Attention 105
    Advocacy for Libraries and Literacy 109
    Celebrations 109
    Working with School and Library Boards 110
    Effective Communication Methods 110

Bibliography 153

Index

Dedication

This book is dedicated with love to my grandchildren Trinity, Ethan, Kira, Julie and the twins, Alexander and Christian.

List of Copyright Permissions Necessary

Sarah Shaw
Olathe School District

Christine Walker
Olathe School District

Acknowledgments

Thanks to all my friends and colleagues who helped me with this project. They shared their talents, time, ideas, and skills to help this book come to fruition. Special thanks go to Pat Conover, Elaine Crider, Charlotte Davis, Kathi Knop, Chris Larson, Jackie Mense, Donna Miller, Peggy Monroe, Leigh Anne Neal, Brad Rankin, Sarah Shaw, Jane Tolman, Christine Walker, and Terry Wintering for their instrumental help and encouragement.

Author Information

Cynthia Anderson is an associate superintendent of schools for a large suburban school district in Kansas. She oversees libraries, instructional television, curriculum and instruction, staff development, career and technical education, virtual school, special education, and federal programs. During her long career in public education, she has been a school librarian, a principal, a director of media services and most recently, associate superintendent. Her first love, after her family, is libraries – advocating for them, working in them and writing about them.

Linworth Publishing published *Write Grants, Get Money*, her first book, in 2002. She has published articles in *Library Media Connection, Knowledge Quest, Library Talk, Reading Teacher, School Library Activities Monthly*, and the *School Librarian's Workshop*. She serves on the editorial review board of the IRA publication *Reading Teacher*.

In her leisure time, Cynthia enjoys her grandchildren and restoring a 19th century stone house in the Flint Hills of Kansas.

Appendices

Appendix A: Copyright Policy 117

Appendix B: Disposal of Materials Procedure 119

Appendix C: Goal Chart 121

Appendix D: Friends of Libraries 123

Appendix E: Architectural Requests 125

Appendix F: Sample Furniture Specifications 129

Appendix G: Linking Literature 135

Appendix H: Instruction to Support Curricular Objectives 139

Appendix I: Indian Creek Brochure 141

Appendix J: Results-Based Staff Development Plan 143

Appendix K: Elementary Library Media Center Monthly Report 145

Appendix L: Secondary Library Media Center Monthly Report 147

Appendix M: Sample Nomination Letter 149

Appendix N: Sample Press Release 151

Table of Figures

Figure 1.1	Sample Elementary Library Staffing Guidelines	10
Figure 2.1	Library Selection Policy	16
Figure 2.2	Assessment Data	22
Figure 2.3	Circulation Statistics	23
Figure 3.1	Holdings by Dewey	33
Figure 3.2	Holdings	34
Figure 3.3	Age of Collection Graph	35
Figure 3.4	Library Budget Allotment	41
Figure 4.1	School Library Allocations	46
Figure 4.2	Budget Per Pupil	47
Figure 4.3	Media Services Profile	49
Figure 5.1	Calculating Necessary Shelving	62
Figure 6.1	Library Monthly Curriculum	81
Figure 9.1	Awards	107
Figure 9.2	Library Brochure	112
Appendix C	Goal Chart	121
Appendix H	Instruction to Support Curricular Objectives	139
Appendix J	Results-Based Staff Development Plan	143

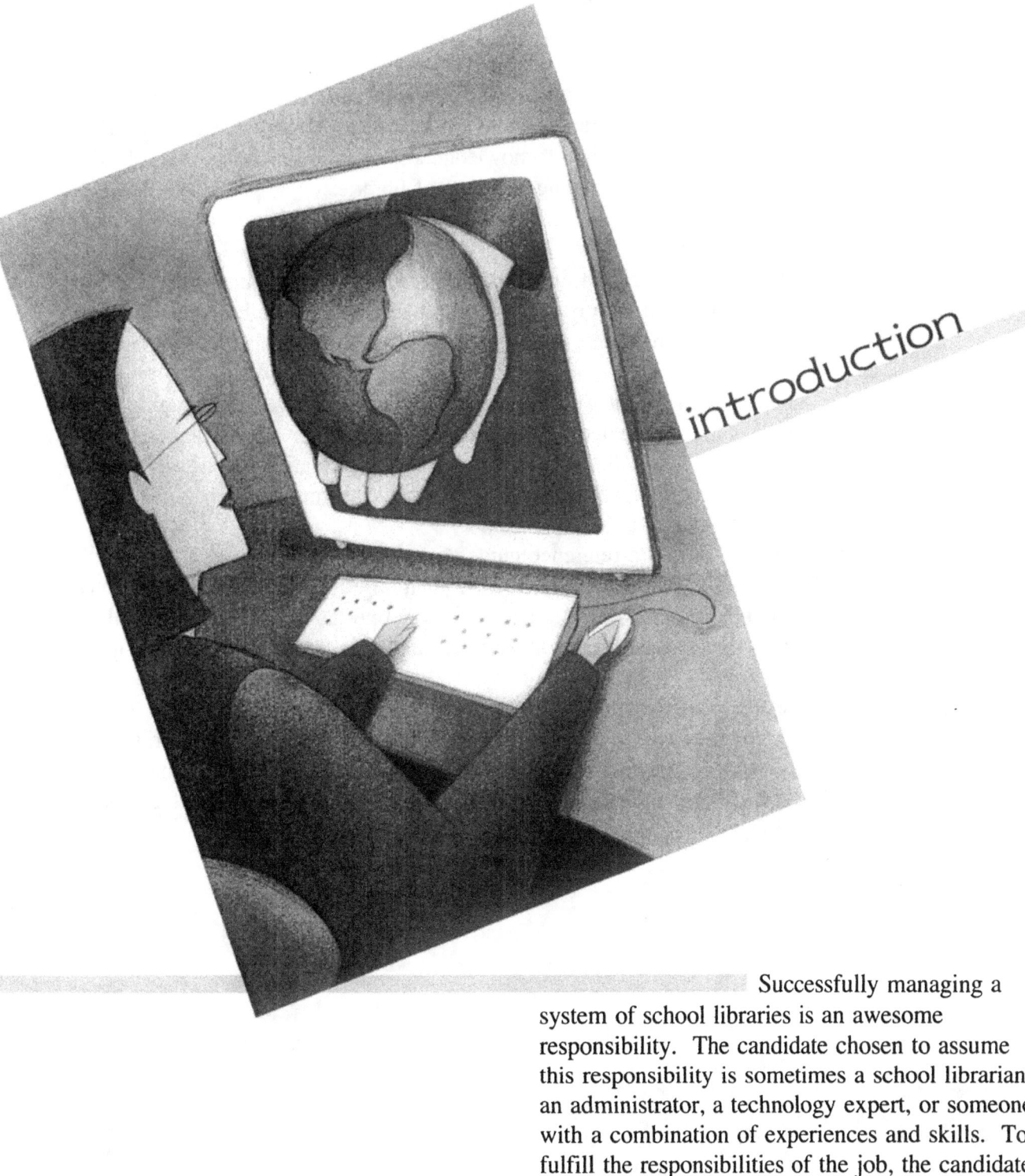

introduction

Successfully managing a system of school libraries is an awesome responsibility. The candidate chosen to assume this responsibility is sometimes a school librarian, an administrator, a technology expert, or someone with a combination of experiences and skills. To fulfill the responsibilities of the job, the candidate will need support and assistance. This book was written to serve as a reference book and a road map for the district library administrator.

The book provides a handbook of responsibilities and tips to help a school library director conquer the job. Each of us has a set of skills and gifts that we bring to the job. Few of us know the answers to all of the questions and possess all of the knowledge required. We can all use a little help from our friends at one time or another. Consider this volume your friendly "go to" helpful source when your job supplies you with an opportunity to stretch your skills. The job of district library administrator is a lonely and isolated one. This book is designed to fill the gap of knowledge and experience that faces each of us as we fill the position of managing a system of libraries.

If you are considering a career as a library media director or have recently been selected to supervise multiple library media centers, then you will find the answers to many questions within the pages of this book. Whether you have been managing multiple libraries for many years, or you are new to the job, or you are planning for a career in library management, you will benefit from the information in this book.

Chances are good that there are not many people in your geographic area who share your job experience. Few opportunities exist for networking and exchanging ideas. You will feel you have ended that isolation when you dive into this volume and get the answers, practical tips, and information you need from your colleagues across the country.

Use this book as a reference guide as questions arise or read it cover to cover for a comprehensive overview of the position of library media director who manages multiple libraries. Either way, you will find hands-on examples of the help you need to solve problems, make plans, and effectively manage your library system.

Use the table of contents and the index to search the topics about which you need more information. Use the appendices for samples of forms, policies, and other concrete examples you may need in your position. This volume covers the topics of staffing, policies, the collection, budgets and fundraising, facilities, programming, technology, professional development, and advocacy.

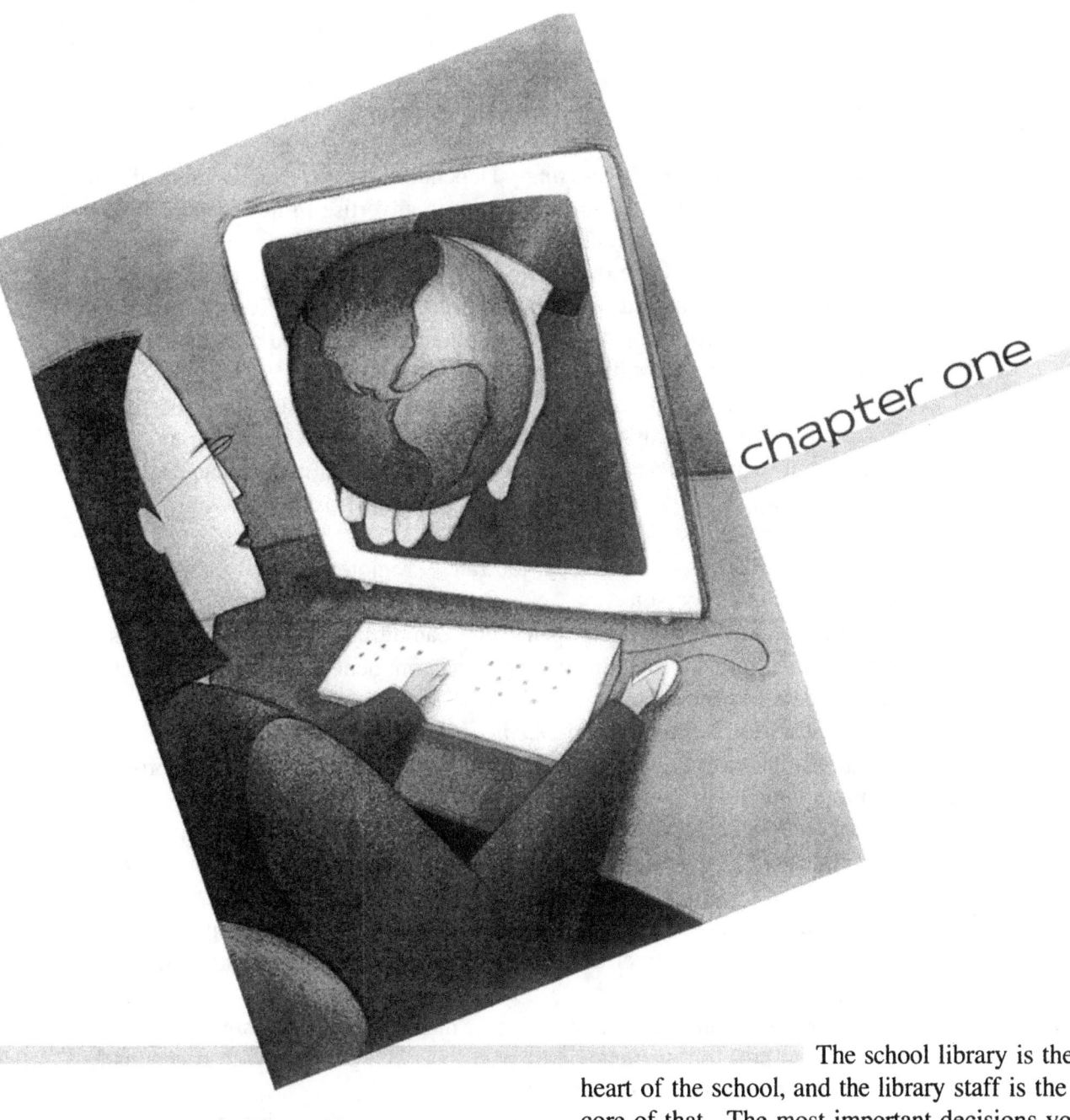

Staffing and Personnel

chapter one

The school library is the heart of the school, and the library staff is the core of that. The most important decisions you will make in your job as library media director are those that involve hiring. People make things happen. Author Jim Collins, in his book *Good to Great*, advises us to decide, "First Who, Then What: Achieving greatness begins with the right team of people; adopting program and business strategies comes later." The same is true for libraries. Choosing people for your team is a delicious opportunity to make your vision of the library program come true.

Recruitment and Screening

There are several ways to recruit new staff members.

- *Job Posting*—If your district has a system of posting jobs internally, you will want to advertise your open library positions on that system.
- *Newspaper or Magazine Advertising*—Depending on the scarcity of candidates and the size of your budget, you may want to advertise in newspapers and or journals to attract highly qualified applicants.
- *Employee Referrals*—Some districts offer a bonus to current employees who recruit a new hire in a hard-to-fill position, like librarians. Even if there is no bonus, ask library employees to refer good candidates. You could set up an internal recognition and public thank you program.
- *School Recruiting*—Visit your area library schools when they have job fairs. Set up a booth and distribute promotional materials about your district. Market your district. Meet with the library information management staff and visit with them about your school district. Offer internships for their students. Volunteer to be a guest lecturer.
- *Job Fairs*—Book a booth at a local job fair. Promote your district and attract viable applicants in person.
- *Open Houses*—A well-planned open house can attract community members. A poster and recruitment materials set up in a prominent display could attract just the candidate you are seeking.
- *Educational TV Channel Advertisement*—If your district has access to an educational channel, put your want ads on bulletin board screens and broadcast them intermittently.
- *Internet Web Page Posting*—Many districts now routinely post job openings on their Web page. Be sure to get your library positions posted on your school district's Web page.
- *Banners and Signs*—There is nothing like a bold *Now Hiring* banner or sign on a school on a busy street to get the word out to the community that you have job openings.
- *Professional Associations*—As a courtesy, many professional organizations allow you to post job openings in their newsletters, on their Web pages, and announce them at professional meetings.
- *Newsletters*—Place job postings in your library and school district newsletters.

There are pros and cons to the different methods that should be considered. Obviously cost and timing are big considerations as well as efficiency. Your human resources department will have procedures in place and preferences for recruiting. Be sure to consult with and work hand-in-hand with them through the hiring process.

Another way to search for applicants is online. Instead of only recruiting and posting your jobs online, go online and search for applicants. Try the following sites for finding library media staff members:

- Council On Library /Media Technicians
    <<http://colt.ucr.edu/ncccjob.html>>
- The Library and Information Science Professional's Career Development Center
    <<www.liscareer.com/>>
- Library Support Staff Resource Center

<<flightline.highline.edu/lssrc/>>
- Resources for on the job in libraries
    <<www.librarysupportstaff.com/libjobs.html>>
- Your Local Newspaper's Web Site

Hiring Laws and Policies

Several laws influence hiring and supervising staff. Awareness of these laws will serve you well. You should be familiar with the following fair employment laws and allow them to guide you.

1. *Affirmative Action*—When *Title VII* of the *Civil Rights Act of 1964* did not have the rapid effect it was hoped for, Executive Order 11246 was given in 1965 by the federal government requiring entities doing business with the federal government to make several commitments. The three most important of those were:
    - Practice nondiscrimination in employment.
    - Obey the rules and regulations of the Department of Labor.
    - Attain affirmative action goals.
2. *Age Discrimination in Employment Act of 1967*—This law protects workers from ages forty to seventy. It was later amended to cover workers older than seventy. Employees should not be discriminated against in matters of pay, benefits, working conditions, or continued employment regardless of how old they are. What matters is their ability to do the job.
3. *Americans With Disabilities Act of 1990*—This law prohibits all employers from discriminating against employees or job candidates with disabilities as long as they can perform the essential functions of the job with or without accommodation. This is a very complex law that requires in-depth understanding.
4. *Children's Internet Protection Act (CIPA)*—This law was enacted to require Internet filters on computers that children might be using in schools and libraries if they accept federal funding.
5. *Civil Rights Act of 1964*—This well-known legislation protects several groups of people and pertains to many employment situations. *Title VII* of this act prohibits discrimination on the basis of race, color, religion, sex, or national origin in employment. It prevents discrimination in hiring, training, promotion, and working conditions. Vietnam veterans were given freedom from discrimination protection in 1974.
6. *Civil Rights Act of 1991*—This law offers more protection and financial remuneration for potential victims of different forms of discrimination.
7. *Consolidated Omnibus Budget Reconciliation Act (COBRA)*—This requires an entity with twenty or more employees who sponsors a group health plan to extend coverage to employees and dependents in situations where employees might otherwise lose coverage.
8. *Drugfree Workplace Act of 1988*—If your school district receives grants from the federal government of $25,000 or more, the district must meet

posting and record-keeping requirements and must have a policy prohibiting the manufacture, distribution, possession, or use of controlled substances in the workplace.

9. *Elementary and Secondary Education Act (ESEA)—Reauthorization—No Child Left Behind*—The 2002 reauthorization of the *ESEA* set restrictions and requirements for highly qualified teachers and for educational assistants and paraprofessionals who provide direct service to students in Title I schools. There are some very stringent requirements in this law regarding the qualifications of these staff members.

10. *Employee Polygraph Protection Act*—The law prohibits the use of polygraph tests in decision making in most pre-employment and employment situations.

11. *Employees Retirement Insurance Security Act (ERISA)*—This governs the protection of pensions and retirements funds including 403(b)s.

12. *Equal Pay Act of 1963*—This act requires that men and women performing substantially equal work receive equal pay.

13. *Fair Labor Standards Act (FLSA) 1938*—This act governs how you pay exempt and non-exempt status employees, and governs overtime, minimum wage, and child labor.

14. *Family and Medical Leave Act of 1993*—*FMLA* allows eligible employees to take a total of twelve weeks leave during any twelve-month period for the birth or adoption of a child, an employee's serious health condition, or the serious health condition or care taking of a spouse, child or parent.

15. *Health Insurance Portability and Accountability Act (HIPAA)*—An act which ensures that employees leaving one employer's health plan have access to the new employer's plan without limitations due to pre-existing conditions. Added in 2002 are restrictions that require the employer to ensure the privacy of the employees' medical information.

16. *Immigration Reform and Control Act of 1986*—It is illegal to hire undocumented immigrants and the employer is required to determine and document an applicant's authorization to work in the United States.

17. *National Origin Discrimination Guidelines*—The employer may not deny equal employment opportunity because of an individual's ancestry; place of origin; or physical, cultural, or linguistic characteristics.

18. *Occupational Safety Health Act (OSHA)*—This law makes sure that employees have a safe and healthy workplace.

19. *Omnibus Budget Reconciliation Act (OBRA)*—Group health plans are required to cover adopted children with no pre-existing condition limitations.

20. *Pregnancy Discrimination Act of 1978*—The *PDA* prohibits discrimination based on pregnancy, childbirth, or related conditions. Women must be allowed to work as long as they can perform the essential elements of their job. The employer cannot enforce a mandatory pregnancy leave. Pregnant job candidates must have equal employment opportunities if they can perform the essential elements of the job.

21. *Rehabilitation Act of 1973*—A section of this act, section 501, prohibits discrimination against people with disabilities by contractors doing $2,500

or more of business per year with the federal government.
22. *Religious Discrimination Guidelines*—The Equal Employment Opportunity Commission (EEOC) offers several guidelines. The 1972 revision of *Title VII* states that an employer must accommodate "all aspects of religious observance and practice, as well as belief, unless an employer demonstrates that he is unable to reasonably accommodate an employee's or prospective employee's religious observance or practice without undue hardship on the conduct of the employer's business."
23. *Unemployment Compensation*—State laws control income for employees whose job loss is due to circumstances beyond their control.
24. *Women's Health and Cancer Rights Act*—This offers specific protection for workers with breast cancer who elect reconstructive surgery in connection with a mastectomy.
25. *Workers Compensation*—States control insurance for employees injured on the job.

Each of these laws has an impact on hiring procedures and decisions. Become familiar with them. Make sure that you are absolutely in compliance with both the letter and spirit of the laws that govern hiring practices.

In addition to the federal laws that govern hiring practices, state and local laws also exist that may dictate some of your procedures and practices. Consider attending a hiring and employment law seminar in your state to learn more.

Job Descriptions

Each position in your department needs a job description. A job description is a formal document, usually in a uniform format that identifies the job and its essential responsibilities. It should be written in a clear and concise manner. The job description has several uses:

- Job Posting—The job description sets the expectations for job functions and responsibilities right from the outset. The potential candidate can do a self-evaluation from reading the job description to assess if she is a viable candidate.
- Interviewing—The job description should be the skeleton around which the interview questions are formed.
- Recruiting—When recruiting, the job description is a shorthand method of describing the position(s) available.
- Performance Appraisals—A well-written job description is the start and end point of a comprehensive performance appraisal. The job description carefully spells out the precise expectations of the job.
- Disciplinary Action—A job description delineates job expectations and provides justification for any disciplinary action that must be taken.

Before writing a job description, you need to perform a careful analysis of the job.

You can do that by:

- Asking for written and verbal input from those who are currently doing or supervising the job you wish to describe
- Observing over time those performing the job
- Sending out questionnaires to those who are in the job and those who supervise it
- Looking at sample job descriptions online

Once you know the tasks that the job entails, you are ready to write the job description. Write concisely using action words. Eliminate unnecessary articles and use the present tense. Make sure all of the requirements are job related and are in accordance with the equal employment opportunity laws and regulations. Include the following in your job description:

- Date
- Job title
- Division or department
- Exemption status
- Salary grade and range
- Work schedule
- Job summary
- Duties and responsibilities
- Equipment to be used
- Desired skills
- Special physical requirements (such as the ability to lift and carry 25 pounds)

Interviewing

Interviewing is a platinum opportunity to get to know potential candidates and to compare their skills, their ability to form positive relationships, and their personalities to the position you are seeking to fill. The interview is the time to determine the fit between the candidate, the job, and the organization or system. According to a Harvard Business School study, more than 75% of job turnover can be attributed to faulty interviewing practices and procedures.

Preparing to Interview

It is prudent to use a structured interview format, as opposed to an unstructured, off the top of your head interview format. The time you spend preparing for an interview is time well spent. It will pay off for you later.

Each position for which you interview needs a formal, structured set of questions and a scoring rubric that scores the candidate's knowledge and skills against the job requirements that are set out in the job description. If you use the scoring rubric, be sure to have a place to assess the chemistry fit to your culture and to others with whom the candidate will be required to work. In other words, you need a set of interview questions for the position of librarian, library clerk or aide, library processor, administrative assistant, and any other that you must fill.

Once you have developed an accurate job description for the position, you will have already determined the skills, abilities, and competencies necessary for that job. Use the relevant set of interview questions with each of the applicants for a particular job opening for reasons of fairness. There are many laws that impact fair interviewing, so a solid set of appropriate, legal interview questions is critical to the appearance and documentation of non-discriminatory and successful hiring. Hiring decisions must be made on actual job qualifications so questions should be restricted to those which will elicit job-related information only.

When you have your set of questions, type them up and leave ample space between the questions so that you can take notes during the interview. When you interview, be sure to let the candidate know that you are using this set of questions for each applicant and that you are taking notes so that when you prepare later to make a decision, you will have an accurate recollection of each candidate's answers. Use your scoring rubric to select the best candidate and keep good employment records.

Behavioral interviewing is an interviewing style that is based on asking questions designed to learn past behaviors in order to best predict future behaviors. Knowing how an applicant has acted in the past is the best predictor available. Rather than asking hypothetical questions, the interviewer asks questions focused on having the candidate describe actions taken in past experiences. To learn this information, the interviewer must structure questions that include three components:

> Situation—Have the applicant describe a past experience.
> Action—Learn what action the candidate took and how he handled the situation.
> Result—What was the result of the applicant's action?

Mixed in with the behavioral questions, the interviewer will also want to combine behavioral questions with factual answers in order to elicit a complete picture of the applicant's skills and experience. Refine your interview questions over time to make sure that you have fair, predictive questions that will help you gain the information you need to make good hiring decisions.

Negotiated Agreements

If your school district has a negotiated agreement with the teachers, part of your job will be making sure that you are abiding by that contract in all that you ask librarians to do. An example of this charge is setting meeting times. If, by contract, your elementary, middle, and high school teachers start and end work at three different times each day, any meetings that you schedule will have to occur during their contract time. Teacher planning time is another negotiated item that you will have to ensure is provided for each librarian. To accomplish this feat of scheduling, you will need to work with building principals.

System Staffing Guidelines

Schools systems typically have a set of staffing guidelines that determine class sizes and the number of sections of students that teachers and librarians can teach. Become familiar with those guidelines, and be prepared to work with human resources staff in assisting with staffing the libraries in the school district.

Figure 1.1

Sample Elementary Library Staffing Guidelines

Number of Sections	Librarians Plus Aide Time
35+	2.0
30 – 34	1.5 + 2 hours
24 – 29	1.0 + 6 hours
19 – 23	1.0 + 3 hours
17 – 18	1.0 + 2 hours
15 – 16	1.0
13 – 14	.6 + 3 hours
11 – 12	.5 + 3 hours
10 or fewer sections	.4 + 3 hours

Staff Evaluation

You may either be the primary evaluator of librarians and library staff or be asked to assist someone, probably the building principal, in the evaluation of them. You may also be asked to serve as a resource person to assist librarians who are on performance improvement plans. Your school district probably has a detailed evaluation system that you must follow. If not, you will need to develop an annual evaluation system. Begin that process by examining evaluation tools of other districts. Call on your colleagues from other districts for samples. For examples, do a search for library evaluation forms on the Internet.

Training Paraprofessionals and Other Non-Certified Staff

You will need a training program for paraprofessionals and other non-certified staff. While you may provide the initial training, if the employee is to be school-based, you will also need to provide site-based training or ensure that training will be held on site. The starting point for developing the training is the job description. Typically new employees are evaluated after ninety days, and then annually after that. See an Internet site like HR.BLR.com for sample classified employee evaluation forms, or do an Internet search for an example of a school district classified employee evaluation form.

Encourage all staff members to set measurable goals as part of the evaluation system. Review these goals annually. Match these goals to the goals in your district's long-range plan, your technology plan, and your library long-range plan.

Certification and Licensure Credentials

You should be familiar with your state's requirements for school library media certification and for licensure and ensure that the library staff has the proper credentials. During recent years, many changes in these rules and regulations have been introduced. Make sure that you can help all of your librarians become and remain highly qualified. The reauthorization of the *Elementary and Secondary Education Act (ESEA), No Child Left Behind*, has put a renewed focus on having all staff members be "highly qualified." See your state department of education to clarify the definition of "highly qualified."

Get to know staff in the licensure section of your state department of education in order to be able to give input into and participate in any changes that might be afoot. Keep in regular contact with them so that you always have current information to pass along to the librarians.

New Staff Orientation and Mentoring Programs

You will find that providing a quality orientation to a new employee is time and energy well spent. From day one, establish the vision, the performance and service expectations, and the climate that you feel is the essence of your organization. Plan ahead, and pay attention to details. The time to start planning for the new employee's orientation is the time when you know the job will be open. Start a folder of important documents and information long before the person is hired. Include in it your weekly staff memos and monthly newsletters, a library calendar, a brochure about your libraries, and other information that will be useful to the new employee. Assemble a staff directory of library employees, maps to the necessary libraries and schools, as well as organizational charts for the school district and the library department.

Will the employee need a pre-ordered ID badge? Will she need business cards? Do not forget to revise the staff directory and library directory to include her information. Provide printed directions to your online library handbook. Establish a routine with your office team that takes care of these tasks each time there is a new hire. Do you have printed directions to access your online library handbook available?

Sit down with the members of your department and make an orientation plan for each of the jobs for which you will be hiring. Write the plan and revise it so that it covers all areas of responsibility. Provide a mentor to the new staff member. There is so much information to digest that it is a good idea to provide short orientation sessions, followed by tours of the appropriate facilities and introductions to colleagues. Make sure the employee's desk is stocked with necessary library supplies.

Get started on the right foot from the beginning. The initial orientation is important to the employee's long-range performance. You will want to form a bond with this person, establish a feeling of inclusion, share the vision, and set the course for the future. Allow plenty of time for orientation, and consider offering several short, meaningful orientation sessions the first few days she is on the job. Plan the sessions ahead of time and know the topics you plan to cover. Have the materials ready and packaged in the order you plan to cover them. Make the sessions short, and then take tours of pertinent areas. Introduce key players to her and schedule short meaningful meetings with the necessary staff members.

This is a magical time to share the core values of the organization. Make sure the new hire leaves each session with increased confidence, pumped up, and ready to hit the ground running. Share the important things that make a difference.

Procedures Manual

Having a procedures manual can make your job as administrator much simpler. An up-to-date, accurate manual can be the backbone of a new employee training program. Having a current procedure manual in process for each of your job descriptions is a good insurance policy for future vacancies. The production of those manuals can be a valuable job target for veteran employees. The time to start developing the manual is before you have the resignation paperwork from a key employee. Although the production of the manual is a big job, it is worthwhile and can be done bit by bit. Asking employees to list and describe the special projects they oversee is one way to start. Another step is to get staff members to list and describe the routine tasks they perform daily in their jobs.

Another way to help with the development of the procedures manual is to cross train employees and have them write as they learn. As the staff member rotates through the various jobs and departments, she can identify critical routines and action steps of the jobs. Moving from processing books, to cataloging, to acquisitions, to shipping, gives an employee a good knowledge of the entire process, builds flexibility in your staff, and can help with the development of the procedures manual.

Assisting Building Principals

Work collaboratively with building-level administrators. There are many ways that you can work together with building principals. You can assist in:

- *Recruiting*—Busy principals appreciate you networking with area library schools, working with human resources, and attracting viable candidates to your school district. Always carry your business cards so that you have a ready handout to possible candidates for your school district's employment.
- *Screening*—Your human resources department probably has a carefully spelled-out screening process. In addition to their screening process, they are probably counting on you to develop and give each library candidate a library screener. This screener can be one that you have developed over time. You need to give the same screener to each candidate, score each answer using a scoring rubric, and keep good records of those scores.
- *Interviewing*—You may be called upon to provide some of the questions for principals to use when they interview library candidates. You may also be invited to sit in on the school interview teams when school staff interviews the candidates. A file of interview questions could come in handy.
- *Hiring*—On some occasions, you may be asked to make hiring decisions for the schools. On those occasions, be sure that you know precisely what the principal and staff are looking for in their new librarian.
- *Providing Orientation*—One of your responsibilities will be to provide orientation for the new librarians. Your orientation will be to the system in general and the job in specific. While the building can provide local orientation and the who, what, when, why and how, much of the orientation to library responsibilities will rest on your shoulders.
- *Developing Programs and Curriculum*—Principals are counting on you to

provide the curriculum and to provide a framework of programs for the local librarian to embellish. They are counting on your support in equipping library media specialists with the skills they need to assist in the fulfillment of the building school improvement plan.

- *Scheduling Classes*—Sometimes the principal needs help with scheduling library classes and will call on you for assistance.
- *Facility Needs*—Principals rely on you to determine many of the physical needs in the library such as when it needs new furnishings, carpet, and paint.
- *Emergency Assistance*—The time will come when you are called upon for emergency assistance in the school. It may be because of a staff relationship problem involving the librarian, it may be a job performance issue, or it may be something simple like assistance in weeding the collection. Be ready to work cooperatively with building administrators.

Working with Other Administrators

In your position of administering libraries, you will need to work cooperatively with your colleagues who administer other facets of the school district. You cannot provide the services your libraries need without the help and assistance of these other district administrators. You must build good working relationships with the people who perform other vital functions for your school district. Trust is the foundation of good working relationships.

- *Superintendent*—Your superintendent is key to the success of your libraries. Give yourself the assignment of building a positive, constructive and solid relationship with the superintendent. Library staffing, funding and programming is directly impacted by the superintendent's attitude toward and working relationship with you. Make sure your work is also seen positively by the community, the school board, and by other administrators.
- *Director of Curriculum and Instruction*—The librarians in your district serve as resource specialists in their buildings. They should know the district curriculum and the state and national curriculum standards well. Work with the person in charge of curriculum and instruction in order to make sure that the librarians are included in curriculum development, textbook selection, and other critical operations of that department.
- *Director of Special Education*—Your colleague who oversees special education is someone with whom you need to work closely. You must ensure that your libraries meet the physical needs of all students as well as their academic needs. The librarians may need your help and understanding as they accommodate the needs of special education students and differentiate instruction in the library.
- *Staff Development Trainer*—Work collaboratively with the person in your district who oversees staff development. Work together to guarantee that the library staff members have the training opportunities necessary to keep their skills current, as well as opportunities to train other district staff.
- *Manager of Operations and Maintenance*—An alliance with this key player will serve you well. As you advocate for the maintenance, remodeling,

rebuilding, refitting, and refurbishing of the school libraries, your relationship with this person can mean all the difference to you. When pipes freeze and libraries flood, or mold attacks your collections, you will be working closely with the maintenance department.

- *Manager of the Business Office*—Libraries routinely purchase materials and keep the business office busy with their purchase orders. Keep the relationship between the business office and the library staff on a smooth course to get the best results for the libraries. Play by their rules and let them know they are appreciated.
- *Technology Director*—No one is more instrumental in your success than the person who oversees technology for your school district. Start on the correct foot with this key player, and work collaboratively for the good of all.

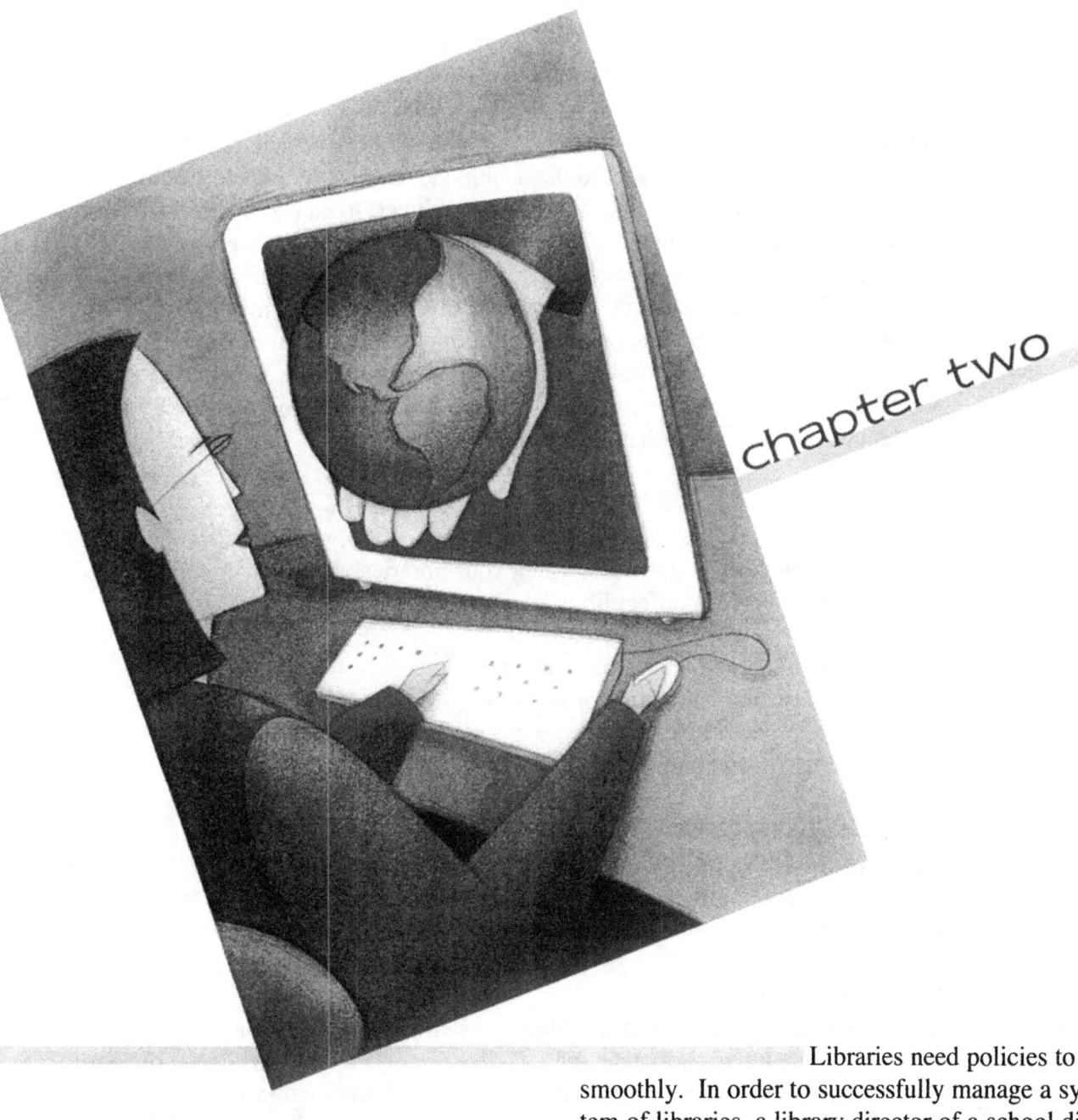

chapter two

Policies and Plans

Libraries need policies to run smoothly. In order to successfully manage a system of libraries, a library director of a school district needs to ensure that policies are in place to meet the challenges and opportunities that libraries encounter. Better to have the policies and know that the school board and administration support them before the actual need for the policies arises. Policies and procedures for school libraries are like insurance policies; by the time you really need one it is usually too late to adopt one. Do not be caught in that position; develop your policies and get them approved by all of the powers that be, well in advance of the day you will actually need to use them. Your staff is relying on you to provide the security of well-written policies that stand the tests that are put to them.

One of the responsibilities of the director of libraries is to identify what policies are needed and to assist in the development of those policies. Efficient policies and procedures are vital to the health and survival of a library system.

From advisory boards, to standing committees, to ad hoc committees, the acceptance and implementation of good policies and procedures are dependent upon the involvement of the stakeholders and users. Be sure that key players buy in to the policies that you adopt. It may take several meetings; many hours of discussion; and much researching, comparing, and contrasting, but getting buy-in from all the stakeholders is critical. Ask each of them to bring ideas to the table. Assign parts of policies for research and suggestions. Work together until you have documents that all of the players feel meet the needs of your school district.

Identifying Necessary Policies

If you are new to your school system or new to your job, you will want to examine the existing policies that govern or affect your libraries. Places that you will need to check for policies that affect libraries are in your existing:

- Board of education policy book
- Library director's or administrator's handbook
- School library media specialist's handbook
- Student policy handbooks

As you examine these documents, check to make sure that you have a comprehensive array of policies that will cover all of your needs. Once you have located and read these documents, take an inventory of existing policies. Do you have the following?

Selection Policy

A selection policy is central to any library system. It will guide the purchase of materials and help the district defend its collection when the collection is questioned. Many districts rely on the American Library Association's tried and true *Library Bill of Rights* as the spine of their selection policy. You can find that policy at <<www.ala.org>>.

The following Figure 2.1, Library Selection Policy, is a sample selection policy that may be a starting place for you to use to develop yours.

Figure 2.1

Library Selection Policy

The policy of the School District is to provide a wide range of learning resources that promote literacy and support the curriculum at varying levels of difficulty and points of view to meet the needs of students and staff members.

Responsibilities for actual selection of school library materials shall rest with the certified school library media specialists who shall discharge this obligation consistent with the Board's adopted selection criteria and procedures. The library media specialists will work cooperatively with staff members and students to interpret and guide the application of the policy in making day-to-day selections.

Gifts to Libraries Policy

People like to give used materials to school libraries. Sometimes we like to receive them. Sometimes people like to give new materials to school libraries. Sometimes the materials are just what you would like to have. Other times the materials may be moldy, outdated, or controversial, and you would very much prefer not to have them in your library system. Sometimes the donors have agendas beyond the simple donation of a book. For these reasons and many more, your school library system needs a gift policy.

Craft your policy carefully so that you can accept the materials you wish to accept and reject those you do not want. Refer to your library selection policy in your gift policy so that gifts meet the same selection criteria as other elements of your collection.

Along with the development and adoption of your policy, you will need procedures for handling donated library materials. Once you have the policy and the procedures, follow them to the letter and handle all donations according to your written policy. Find a sample gift policy and some guidelines online at www2.lindbergh.k12.mo.us/lmsc/gift.PDF or search your state's board of education Web site for samples.

Objectionable Materials Complaint Policy

Concerns or complaints about objectionable materials must eventually appear in most libraries. No library media center is immune to the occasional complaint or concern. They may range from a concern from a kindergarten parent about the implied violence in *Flopsy, Mopsy, and Cottontail* to a high school parent's concern with the language in *I Know Why the Caged Bird Sings*. Most of these concerns can be resolved easily with a conference between the parent or patron and the library media specialist. Often a parent simply wants reassurance that her child will select materials for checkout that will match that family's values and beliefs. A few concerns, however, cannot be resolved that easily. For those that cannot be resolved with a simple conference, a policy and a procedure can be a tremendous benefit for all of the parties.

When the concern becomes a complaint or a formal objection you will need a policy. Along with the policy, you will need procedures for handling this type of situation. A sample of one school district's procedures for handling a formal complaint can be found online at www1.smsd.org/boeweb/KEC-E.htm.

Copyright Policy

Following the U.S. and international copyright laws is crucial to operating both a library and a school system. Librarians are looked upon as the local school district's authorities on copyright law. The school district is vulnerable to charges of copyright violations. The copyright laws are complex and subject to interpretation. For these reasons and for many others, it is imperative to have and abide by an effective copyright policy. An example of a short and to-the-point policy can be found in Appendix A.

Online resources are available for information about copyright and fair use. These resources are appropriate for staff development.

- A Teacher's Guide to Fair Use and Copyright
  <<http://home.earthlink.net/~cnew/research.htm>>
- Hall Davidson's Copyright Resources
  <<www.mediafestival.org/downloads.html>>
- *unitedstreaming* Copyright Quiz
  <<http://school.discovery.com/quizzes22/riddlen/CopyrightQuiz.html>>
- The University of Texas System's "Fair Use of Copyrighted Materials"
  <<www.utsystem.edu/OGC/IntellectualProperty/copypol2.htm>>
- Copyright Website
  <<www.benedict.com>>
- Copyright with CyberBee
  <<www.cyberbee.com/cb_copyright.htm>>

Copyright Procedures

In addition to a strict copyright policy, school districts or systems also need guidelines and procedures to follow. Employees, especially in a school district, need to have questions answered and examples given for the many different scenarios involving copyright. Questions abound in school districts about the appropriate use of videos, off-air taping, public performances, and video or audio recordings of school plays. There are many resources to assist you as you write procedures and guidelines. One of the best resources for copyright information is the Carol Simpson book, *Copyright for Schools: A Practical Guide, Third Edition*, published by Linworth Publishing, Inc.

A district would do well to provide some type of copyright procedure manual for students and employees. This is an area that can cost a district mightily if employees are violating the law and the district has not taken the proper steps to ensure that employees are following the law. In many districts the responsibility for writing, publishing, and overseeing the district copyright manual falls on the shoulders of the director of library media services.

A district also needs to be sure that all equipment that can be used to duplicate copyrighted materials is labeled with a warning to staff to follow the copyright laws. A standard way to do this is to produce stickers and make sure they are stuck to computers, photocopiers and other equipment that staff might use for duplication. The typical warning is usually stated something like this.

Copyright Materials

It is the intent of the Board of Education to adhere to the provisions of the US Copyright Laws (Title 17. United States Code. Section 101). Unauthorized reproduction and/or use of copyright materials is illegal and unethical. Violation of the copyright laws may result in criminal or civic suits and/or appropriate disciplinary action for the school district.

Disposal of Materials Policy

Weeding is an integral part of the routine of almost every library, but disposing of those materials you have weeded can cause grief if you do not have a good policy and procedure for their disposal. You never want to see a letter to the editor in your local paper from a patron who is complaining that you claim your libraries need more funding while you are throwing perfectly good books like *Will We Get To The Moon?* in the trash dumpster behind one of your school libraries. No one wants bad press. There should be a convenient and safe way to dispose of materials that are obsolete, worn out, and outmoded, and solid criteria for determining those conditions.

A board adopted policy may exist covering disposal of materials under which you might tuck disposal of library materials. Read your board policies before writing new ones, just in case you can simply modify an existing policy to include your needed library materials disposal policy. An example of a broader school board policy covering disposal of materials, including library materials can be found at http://www1.smsd.org/boeweb/DN.HTM. There should also be specific procedures to follow as was stated previously. See Appendix B for a sample procedure.

Developing Effective Policies

If you find that you do not have these policies and you determine that you need them, you will want to do some research to find examples of other school districts' or systems' policies. You can learn a lot by reading the policies of others. The National School Board Association is a good resource, as are neighboring school districts as you do your research.

Take notes or highlight the attributes of the policies that you particularly like or dislike. Contact your colleagues in other districts or systems and talk with them about their library policies. Get a copy of the ALA's *Library Bill of Rights* and examine it to determine what conflict and compatibilities your existing policies have with it.

Policy Development Process

Library Advisory Committee

Once you have done your research, you will probably want to involve the stakeholders in developing the policies. Stakeholders might include representatives from elementary, middle, and high schools; paraprofessionals or aides; central library processing staff; teachers; administrators; students; and parents. Consider establishing a standing library advisory committee that will be responsible for developing library policies. The library advisory committee could meet quarterly to give advice and counsel to the library director. The library advisory committee could be composed of librarians who represent the elementary, middle, and high schools in your school district. The director should develop the agenda for the meetings and chair them.

Once a draft of a policy is developed, as director, you should take it to your supervisor first for approval. If there is no formal procedure for this process, you must request that your supervisor submit it to the superintendent for approval or revision. If the superintendent approves, it should then be presented to the school board for action.

The board of education will read and discuss the policy. Sometimes they make suggestions for modification of the policy before approving it. You will want to be present at the meeting when the school board reviews and takes action on your policy. Be prepared to answer questions school board members might have. Following approval of the policy, you will need to put a plan in place to communicate the policy to all of the librarians and others who will be affected by it.

Ensuring Compliance With and Implementation of Policies

Another responsibility of a library director is to monitor the compliance with and implementation of school board policies. The library director must:

- Distribute and communicate the policies
- Interpret the policies
- Check for understanding with the policy users
- Ensure adherence and compliance of all staff with the polices
- Provide support to librarians as they implement the policies
- Produce materials and programs for librarians to use in the buildings with the staffs
- Update policies as needed

If, for instance, your school board has a policy for the disposal of school district property, including discarded library materials, it is the responsibility of the director to teach and interpret the policy and to monitor the libraries to make sure that the policy is being followed. If the policy says that discarded materials must be sold at public auction, then part of your job is to ensure that that happens. While donating the discarded items to a local charity might be the preference of a librarian, the school board policy must be followed. The library media director is also charged with the responsibility of making sure that all of the librarians understand the policy, the rationale for it, and that they follow the policy.

Developing a Handbook for Librarians

A well written, well thought-through handbook will facilitate the smooth running of all of the district libraries. It is difficult for all librarians to "be on the same page" if there is no "same page" or handbook that outlines the basic policies, procedures, and information that all of the librarians need to be aware of and share. You may find that your library system conducts business in ways that are traditions, but that the traditions or norms are not written anywhere. This may work if the staff stays the same forever, but staff changes are inevitable, whether it is a new librarian, clerk, or administrator. The district library media team deserves a handbook that will serve all the team members and possibly save you from a few inquiring phone calls from staff.

Just as Rome was not built in a day, the handbook will not spring from your word processor in a few days' time. The handbook may evolve over a year or two, but there is no time like the present moment to start writing and assembling it. To post the handbook online, begin by adding one section at a time.

Sections of the Handbook

Make a folder, and begin to put a spare copy of items that might be appropriate in your handbook into the folder. As you put aside pages, you will begin to see sections of your handbook developing. Consider including the following sections in your handbook:

- Table of Contents—Keep this section current so that users can find the information they are seeking.
- Index—Make sure that you have a comprehensive, up-to-date index in your handbook. The handbook is useful only if the users can find what they are looking for.
- Calendar—Maintain a full year calendar of library and other school events, such as conference days, and school improvement staff development days. Note the dates, times, and locations of all library committee meetings and staff development opportunities for the year on your library calendar.
- Rosters—In the roster section of your library handbook, include alphabetical lists of your schools, the librarians, the library aides, the phone and fax numbers for the libraries, the email addresses of the librarians and clerks, and the school I.D. numbers or codes for interlibrary loan purposes. Also include lists of district library committees with the members' names, meeting dates, times, and locations.
- Assessment—Test scores are of interest to librarians, so you may want to keep librarians informed of their students' scores on the applicable tests, particularly the sections to which the instruction from librarians contribute. For example, if your district gives the Iowa Test of Basic Skills to third and sixth grade students, extract the scores for the reference skills and reading sections of that test. Provide those to the librarians in charts showing several years' history for each school. The following Figure 2.2, Assessment Data, is an example of a chart showing one way to keep track of assessment data history.

Chapter Two: Policies and Plans

Figure 2.2

Assessment Data
School Norms

	3rd Grade			6th Grade		
	Maps & Diagrams	Reference Materials	Total	Maps & Diagrams	Reference Materials	Total
District						
1994/95	83	77	80	89	88	88
1995/96	84	82	84	87	87	87
1996/97	86	83	86	87	88	88
1997/98	88	82	86	89	88	88
1998/99	88	87	89	90	90	89
1999/00	88	88	89	90	91	90
2000/01	89	88	90	92	91	91
2001/02	85	84	85	85	85	86
2002/03	95	98	99	91	92	93
School A						
1994/95	87	78	85	99	90	97
1995/96	89	85	89	99	84	93
1996/97	76	73	75	70	78	74
1997/98	82	63	75	81	79	80
1998/99	99	97	99	96	94	95
1999/00	89	72	84	84	90	87
2000/01	69	79	74	84	80	82
2001/02	74	77	75	80	76	78
2002/03	94	99	98	76	82	80

- Authors—If you have an active visiting author program, all of the information on hosting an author visit can be included in the author section of your handbook. In addition, you may wish to include a list of local or regional authors and illustrators as well as their contact information.
- Bibliography—This section of the handbook offers a sample bibliographic format for librarians at each level. Reading/language arts teachers and librarians should agree on the bibliographic format that you would teach students
- Budgets—Charts showing suggested allocations for library budget expenditures can be provided as a reference for librarians. Each school's library budget can also be provided in this section for the building librarian.
- Curriculum—Include the information literacy and library skills curriculum for each grade level, as well as an outline of the skills that are tested at each grade level, if appropriate.
- Periodicals—Give information about the professional journals and periodicals to which your district subscribes in this section. Also provide information on how to get on the routing slip to read particular journals each month. Include for specific librarians search strategies for the online resources to which your district subscribes.

- Policies and Procedures—Provide pertinent extracts from your board of education policy manual. Examples of the policies and procedures to consider including are copyright, objectionable materials, disposal of district materials and equipment, and gift policies. Some procedures, which are not necessarily policy, can also be described such as weeding, closed captioning methods, and checking in new materials.
- Reading Promotion—This section of the handbook can include many good ideas. From examples of how to conduct book clubs, birthday book clubs, battles of the books, to how to celebrate Children's Book Week, Teen Read Week, National Library Week, and Read Across America, this section should be rich in resources for the librarian. How to instructions for conducting summer library and sustained silent reading can also included in this section.
- Statistics—Circulation statistics provide important information to librarians and other school staff members. Circulation data is often used as one of the measurements for reading improvement on school improvement plans. Provide monthly feedback to all librarians on their circulation. Collect the annual circulation data, and put that into charts that you share with the schools. Figure 2.3, Circulation

Figure 2.3

Circulation Statistics

SCHOOL NAME	POP.	SEPTEMBER			OCTOBER		
		TOTAL CIRC	CIRC/ DAY	CIRC/ STUDENT	TOTAL CIRC	CIRC/ DAY	CIRC/ STUDENT
ELEMENTARY							
School A	295	2640	91.0	8.9	1777	93.5	6.0
School B	130	1667	57.5	12.8	1223	64.4	9.4
School C	360	5516	190.2	15.3	3696	194.5	10.3
School D	612	6404	220.8	10.5	4601	242.2	7.5
School E	541	6980	240.7	12.9	5350	281.6	9.9
School F	302	3399	117.2	11.3	2602	136.9	8.6
School G	575	5735	197.8	10.0	3332	175.4	5.8
School H	653	8142	280.8	12.5	4733	249.1	7.2
School I	405	4886	168.5	12.1	3071	161.6	7.6
School J	367	7300	251.7	19.9	5404	284.4	14.7
School K	243	2974	102.6	12.2	2578	135.7	10.6
School L	379	3158	108.9	8.3	2574	135.5	6.8
School M	336	5071	174.9	15.1	3491	183.7	10.4
School N	340	3394	117.0	10.0	3095	162.9	9.1
School O	330	7166	247.1	21.7	4845	255.0	14.7
School P	303	4671	161.1	15.4	3085	162.4	10.2
School Q	285	4875	168.1	17.1	3241	170.6	11.4
School R	551	6443	222.2	11.7	4529	238.4	8.2
School S	331	3430	118.3	10.4	2286	120.3	6.9

Statistics, shows one way of portraying that information.

- Selection—Include information on selection and a reference to the selection policy for the librarians.

Chapter Two: Policies and Plans

- Collection Development—Provide any documents that you have developed on collection development. This information will help direct new library media specialists and those who are seeking answers to collection development questions.

You may also wish to include per pupil expenditures from year to year.

Handbook Format

You can have an actual hard-copy handbook, or you can have a virtual, or online handbook. The choice is yours. It is easier to update the online version, but some librarians find it easier to consult a physical hard copy. Another option could be to have some of your information online and have a hard copy of the other sections.

For example, if you run a monthly analysis of the average copyright date of a particular Dewey classification for each collection, you probably want to send that report out to librarians in hardcopy and request that they place it in their library handbooks. If you run the report each month on a different Dewey classification, it might not be feasible to post the reports each month online. They may get better attention if sent from you to the librarians in hardcopy.

Be sure to keep your handbook up-to-date, and get feedback from the librarians about what is helpful, clear, and accurate, and what is not. Make revisions annually based on that feedback.

Team Building

Another of the responsibilities or opportunities that falls on the shoulders of the director of the library media program is to build a cohesive team. It is the author's personal belief that the way you get results is through people. People are our most valuable resource in any organization. People all working together for common goals is a powerful organizational dynamic that does not happen accidentally. The leader is the foundation of a cohesive and healthy team. In addition, it takes time and patience. Let's look at a few of the things you can do to start building a team or to strengthen an existing team.

Time

Do not expect to build a team overnight. Building trust takes time. Do not walk in the door to your new job as library director and begin making significant changes if you can possibly avoid it. First, you need to take time to see how the system works, what the positive and not-so-positive attributes of it are, and where the impediments to achieving your vision might be.

Take the time you need to meet the people who work in the libraries; take the time you need to get to know them as people. Take librarians out to breakfast or out for coffee one by one, and get to know them as human beings. Begin to build relationships. Seek to understand. Listen with both ears open and your mouth closed. Remember what Grammy always said: "Act in haste; repent in leisure."

Leadership

The leader cannot just "talk the talk;" the leader must "walk the walk." If you want librarians to treat each and every library "customer" as though they were the children or close relative of the superintendent of schools, then that is how you must treat each library employee. Equity is an issue. You cannot be pleasant to librarians and haughty to the library clerks and expect to be respected. Just a few things the leader can do to set the tone for the team are:

- Appreciate the things that your employees do and let them know it.
- Send heartfelt emails and thank you notes when you see things that employees are doing that are compatible with your core values and vision.
- Give public praise anytime you can, but only if you really mean it.
- Be sincere. When you are thinking a complimentary thought, share it.
- Save your criticisms, if you can, as you build a team.
- Praise in public; redirect in private.

Criticism rarely gets the results we hope for. Teach and redirect instead of criticizing. Focus on the future when redirection is necessary.

Here is a short list of Do's and Don'ts for when you are new in a library leadership position.

Do	**Do Not**
Compliment	Criticize
Listen	Talk too much
Be genuine	Be a fake
See the good in people	Pick on people or be judgmental
Ignore the shortcomings	Nit pick
Use your best manners	Be rude
Smile	Roll your eyes
Look for what is right	Look for what is wrong

Patience

Everybody is different; everybody has strengths. The world would be no fun if we were all alike. Each of your library media employees is a unique and special person with gifts to share with your team. Each one is a jewel. Patience and listening will help you find the special gift and sparkle within each of your employees. We are famous for warning our patrons not to judge a book by its cover. We have to be careful that we do not judge our library media employees or form first impressions that we cannot get past. Working together, honoring one another, being a good listener and having patience will help you build a strong team of eager contributors. We tend to get what we expect we will get. Eager contributors and people with a shared vision can accomplish great goals working together.

Strategic Planning

A system of libraries needs a long-range plan. You may wish to consider strategic planning for your system if you are a large system of libraries. If so, involve your entire team in the process if you want them to buy in and implement the plan and goals. Strategic planning is also one way to get to know your team members better. The steps of strategic planning are simple, but the job requires a time commitment up front and a good facilitator.

Strategic planning will help you paint the big picture and plan for contingencies. How can your system of libraries accomplish your objectives if the team members have not seen the big picture? Having a big picture plan will help your team see what the end result looks like and help them feel secure in their roles and in the day-to-day decisions they must make.

The Steps of Strategic Planning

Step 1
Decide To Plan—Whom do you need to involve? How much time can you dedicate to planning? Where and when will the planning process take place? What period of time do you want the plan to cover? Three to five years is typical. That gives you enough time to accomplish meaningful, long-range goals, but puts you back in the planning mode just in time to keep in front of change. These decisions need to be made as the first step of the strategic planning effort. Does your district have a strategic or long-range plan? If so, for what period of time? Always keep in mind the overall district long-range plan and make the library plan dovetail with the district plan.

Step 2
Assign Responsibilities for the Planning Process—Who will facilitate the planning process? The task sometimes falls to someone outside of your department, but usually it is the task of the library media director. Can you get a local planning consultant to donate facilitation time? Who will write up the recommendations and results of the planning process and to whom will you report it? Who will implement which parts of the plan? When will the recommendations be needed? Will this process require money? If so, where will the money come from? You may need to prepare a timeline placing your normal school year's activities on the plan first, and then work in the extras from the planning process. Who will monitor and evaluate the team's performance and update the plan?

Step 3
Develop or Review your Statement of Purpose (Mission Statement)—This should be a simple statement of the purpose of your system of libraries. It should reflect the core values of the library program. Do not make it too complex or fancy. What is your overarching purpose? Brainstorm together with your team and identify key words, phrases, and ideas. Massage the ideas expressed until you have a succinct expression of your *raison d'etre* or main purpose.

Step 4
Assess Where You Are—Your planning team must ask several questions about your organization or system such as:

- What is the current perception of your library system? What do the

faculty, students, administrators, board members and parents think of your library system? Should you survey them? If so, who will design the survey and analyze the results? Will you need to write a grant to fund this or can it be designed and reevaluated internally?
- Who are your "clients?" Taxpayers? Students? Staff?
- What do you want to do for your clients? How will the clients know you have done something for them?
- What are your opportunities?
- What problems must you overcome?
- What are your strengths and weaknesses?
- What obstacles can you see in the future that will impact your library system?

Another method that works for assessment is the SWOT process in which you identify:

- Strengths – What is working for your system?
- Weaknesses – What areas need improvement?
- Opportunities – What opportunities might be on the horizon?
- Threats – What issues are out there that might pose threats to your organization?

Once you have identified these, develop a plan based on this information. This simple method can work well.

Step 5
What Are Your Needs/Goals?—Make your goals general statements of what you intend to do. The goals should be:

- Results-oriented
- Realistic
- Achievable
- Clear
- Specific
- Measurable
- Flexible
- Time-bounded (steps set out on a realistic school year timeline)
- Assignable
- Supportive of the fulfillment of the mission of your library system

Step 6
Set the Individual Objectives—Look again at your mission statement, your opportunities, your potential obstacles, and your survey or assessment. Define the gaps between your mission and your current assessment. These gaps should help you define your objectives for the period of the plan. What are your most pressing issues and concerns? Prioritize them and name the specific results you want to

accomplish. You may wish to consider several types of objectives:

> *Management*—An example might be a succession plan including staff members acquiring degrees and experiences.
>
> *Service*—Your objective might be for high school librarians to increase the number of times they plan collaboratively with classroom teachers or the number of times English classes do research in the library.
>
> *Expansion/contraction/relocation*—Your objective might be to offer expanded hours in the library during finals week at the end of the semesters.
>
> *Improvement of image, library use, student achievement and test scores.*—For example, you may wish to set a goal of increasing circulation by 5 or 10% for the school year.
>
> *Problem-solving/conflict resolution training*—In a setting where two librarians share a job, you might set the objective to provide conflict resolution training for them in order to reduce interpersonal friction and increase harmony.

Decide how you will measure the accomplishment of the objectives and the goals. Will it be a reduction of staff turnover? Will it be an increase in positive feedback from your patrons or added educational opportunities for staff members?

Step 7

Design The Program—What is it going to take to accomplish this plan? What must you do in year one, year two, etc? It is time to calculate the budget of dollars, time, and resources for each desired outcome. Once you have this information, make a table or outline document that will clearly show the plan.

Step 8

Develop an Action Plan—Make a specific plan. To reach the goals, what do you have to do? Assign the tasks and set the deadlines. Plan what happens if this goal is not met. Go through each goal one by one and decide:

- Who
- What
- When
- Where
- How

Indicate the "to do's" to accomplish for this year, or move the goal to the following year.

Be sure to get approval for your plan from your supervisor before you consider the task complete. In fact, check in with your supervisor after each step of the planning process in order to secure buy-in and support. Do not wait until the end of the process. Garner support each step of the way to ensure a cohesive approach to the plan.

Step 9

Monitor and Evaluate — You and the members of your strategic planning team need to decide how you will communicate your plans, keep them on track and evaluate the progress that you are making. Meet regularly to monitor and report progress.

Tactical Planning

If you are supervising a smaller system of libraries, you may find it easier and more fitting to do tactical planning as opposed to strategic planning. This type of planning requires a smaller team, fewer meetings, and is less complicated. Seminars on tactical planning are offered around the country. Check your mail for fliers on the various seminar companies that offer one-day classes on this topic.

Some of the features of tactical planning are:

- Breaks down an action plan into a time line
- Planning is just for the current year
- Gathers up all of the parts of a plan or process so that nothing is overlooked
- Addresses one need or problem at a time

Tactical planning can be the answer to maintaining the libraries when staffing and funding are in short supply. Decide what the important goals for the year should be and focus on those. Brainstorm with staff and work together to come up with goals that you can accomplish in a year with the resources and staff that you have. For each goal, brainstorm all of the tasks that must be accomplished in order to meet that goal.

Use the chart in Appendix C to plot when, how, and who will get this extra work accomplished for the year. List all of the regular ongoing work on the chart first, including the time of year it occurs. Then fill in the tasks you have set for your team during tactical planning. An example might be that you are going to write a grant for some additional funding. Working backward from the grant submission deadline, project which components of the grant will need to be completed by which dates and fill that in on your chart.

Use multiple copies of the chart so that each member of the planning team can personalize the chart to his own tasks and dates. As the supervisor or overseer, you will keep copies of each team member's chart as well as your own. If you have enough librarians, have them form teams of two or three to get the various goals or components of the goals accomplished.

The Collection: Selection, Purchasing, Ordering, Cataloging, and Processing Materials

chapter three

Planning for, tending, and evaluating the school library collections are some of the nuts and bolts tasks of your job. There are certain decisions you need to make, policies to write, and plans to make in order to help your system function efficiently.

Selection Policy

A selection policy will serve your school library media system well. It is the basis for collection development and the support that you need when you face objections from the community. The policy should ensure that the trained professionals select the library materials. The policy should include all materials such as library books, periodicals, media and textbooks. See *Chapter 2*, Figure 2.1, Selection Policy, for a sample selection policy.

The librarian is trained to select materials. The teachers, administrators, parents and students may share opinions and make recommendations, but the selection remains in the hands of the librarian when you have a strong selection policy. The librarian knows the curriculum, the needs of the staff and students, and the available resources. The librarian knows the materials that are age- and curriculum-appropriate. When in doubt, the librarian can use standard selection tools or other resources. A solid selection policy is helpful when special interest groups exert pressure on your schools.

Collection Development

To run smoothly, a system of school libraries needs a collection development plan. The plan may include policy or maybe just procedures. The preferred way for librarians to develop the collection is by reading reviews and ordering materials that have been favorably reviewed. As the librarian reads the reviews, he should consider:

- Who wrote the review? Teacher? Librarian? Children's author?
- Does the reviewer rate the item highly or give it a starred review?
- Does the item sound interesting?
- Would the item fill a void or do you have other items on that topic?
- Does the item fit the curriculum?
- Does the item represent a diverse point of view?

Review Sources

Librarians need review sources in order to make educated decisions about materials selection. Some review sources available for school librarians are:

- Booklinks: Connecting Books, Libraries, and Classrooms
  <<http://www.ala.org/BookLinks/>>
- Booklist
  <<http://www.ala.org/booklist/index.html>>
- BookSpot
  <<http://www.bookspot.com/>>
- Bulletin of the Center for Children's Books
  <<http://www.lis/ulcuc.edu/puboff/bccb/>>
- Horn Book Magazine
  <<http://www.hbook.com/mag.shtml>>
- LIBRARY MEDIA CONNECTION (LMC)
  <<http://www.linworth.com/lmc.html>>
- MultiMedia Schools Magazine
  <<http://www.infotoday.com/MMSchools/>>
- School Library Journal
  <<http://www.slj.com/>>

A comprehensive review should include information on what the book is about, the target age group, the quality of illustrations, the accuracy of the information, and the author's credentials. The librarian may want to know if controversial topics such as sex, violence, or drugs are included and how those topics are handled. The librarian will probably also want to know if there is raw language before deciding if the item would be a good fit for the students or community.

If you allow librarians to select materials, regardless if they are favorably reviewed or not, a solid roadmap or collection development plan should be in place. Librarians should clearly understand the plan and be able to evaluate their selection choices based on the collection development criteria that have been agreed upon.

Vendor's Recommendations—Caveat emptor! Some vendors have lists of recommended materials that can be helpful, but beware. Not all of the recommended titles are worthy, age-appropriate, or will weather the test of time.

Publisher's Catalogs—These catalogs are normally well indexed and easy for librarians to use to find books, but the purpose of these catalogs is to sell books so they are not reliable selection tools.

Peers' Recommendations—As librarians meet together, they exchange ideas and recommendations for tried and true selections.

Title Lists—Several journals offer annual lists of "bests" that librarians can use as suggested titles.

Make a long-range plan about what areas of the collection need development, prioritize the order in which areas need to be developed, and define the budget process to get the necessary resources. Developing or creating a comprehensive plan that reflects the needs of all of your patrons is a large order. Seek input from your library advisory committee about collection needs. Figure 3.1, Holdings by Dewey, shows one way to document the collection status in your district.

Figure 3.1

| \multicolumn{10}{c}{**Holdings by Dewey**} |
SCHOOL NAME	POP.	TOTAL ITEMS	000	300	500	600	700	900	92
ELEMENTARY									
School A	340	12918	269	829	1354	717	799	767	503
School B	406	17637	310	1199	1687	802	785	1183	1139
School C	505	26669	128	1560	1828	1094	1248	1453	1135
MIDDLE SCHOOLS									
School A	511	14146	117	1037	766	898	878	2314	1669
School B	604	17235	76	1030	658	765	784	1148	1102
School C	617	21949	239	1913	1317	1602	1302	2490	1969
HIGH SCHOOLS									
School A	2086	15638	167	1010	416	412	817	1821	1051
School B	1903	48727	368	4932	1631	3501	3973	5119	2835
School C	1751	27603	187	3834	1242	1720	1691	3298	1360

While you will probably have a district-wide library advisory committee to help with the district collection development plan, each school may also want to have a media advisory committee (MAC). The school's media advisory committee can consist of teachers from the various grade levels and subjects. It could also include student and parent representatives. The principal usually appoints the committee members and the librarian typically chairs the committee. This is a viable way to get input on collection development.

Collection Analysis

One way to begin to produce a collection development plan is to do a complete analysis of the materials your libraries currently have. One of the first things you want to know about each collection is its size. Your automated circulation software system can provide a report of the total number of items in each individual collection as well as the number of items by Dewey classification and other categories. Once you know the size of each of the collections, compare them to state and national standards. Some states prescribe a specific number of titles per student; others specify a number of items according to the size of the school. When analyzing collection size and comparing it to standards, do not include in the count the textbooks or multiple copies of classroom novels or other materials that might be stored in the library. The size of the collection matters, but not if the collection is outdated and obsolete. Involve the librarians in this analysis process.

Figure 3.2

				Holdings			
SCHOOL NAME	POP.	TOTAL ITEMS	A/V	FICTION	NON-FICTION	OTHER	Total Circ by School (Sept-May)
ELEMENTARY							
School A	285	16825	432	7608	6461	2324	25,953
School B	246	17101	831	8080	7375	815	13,108
School C	654	17690	655	7015	8083	1937	44,435
MIDDLE SCHOOLS							
School A	600	20647	1012	4482	9243	5910	14,681
School B	777	15095	601	4292	7202	3000	13,551
School C	1029	19365	1274	4722	12770	599	11,944
HIGH SCHOOLS							
School A	1980	27654	1613	5983	19215	843	9,199
School B	1751	27404	1891	4736	20729	48	13,518
School C	2047	36011	1736	6580	25668	2027	6,106

Next, analyze each collection by subject matter and by copyright date. Most automated management systems will allow you to sort your collections by copyright date and print those copyright date reports. Produce pie or bar graphs of that data to give you a visual look at the average date of the material in the collection. Find an example in Figure 3.3, Age of Collection Graph.

Figure 3.3

Age of Collection Graph

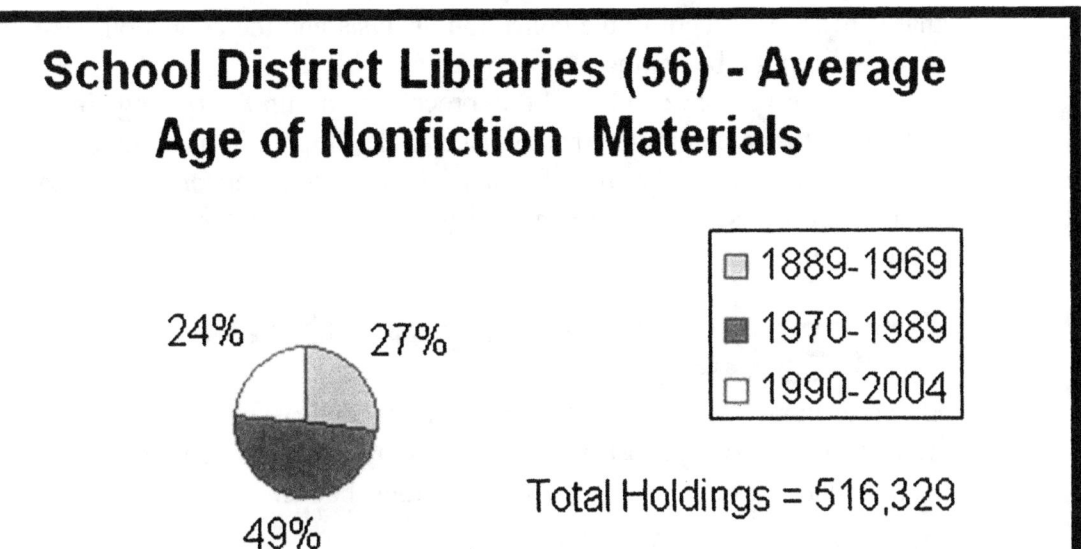

Determine what materials support the curriculum and where there are gaps. Take your curriculum guides and list the topics covered at each grade level and course. Study the textbooks and make charts of the suggested resource materials by grade level, subject and course. Note the Dewey classification on your chart for each subject that you list. Examine the fiction and easy titles that support the curricular subjects.

Evaluate each collection using quality standards. Many factors contribute to make a quality resource. From the reputation of the author/illustrator, to the accuracy of the information, to the literary merit, there are many factors to examine. Is the resource appropriate to the intended grade level? Is the information current, will it remain current, or will it soon become obsolete? Is the durability or construction of the resource a quality you count on? Is the appeal of the resource to your patrons an important quality? Develop criteria based on sound practice when you perform a qualitative evaluation of a collection.

Suggest areas where the collection should be weeded and discarded. Focus on the quality of the materials as opposed to the quantity of materials. Make lists of areas where the collection needs to be developed and then prioritize those lists. Calculate the budget necessary to acquire those materials. If you use the average cost of a book for the elementary level at $20, you can begin to calculate the necessary budget. According to the Texas State Library, the exemplary school library with an enrollment exceeding 600 must provide a minimum of 20 items per student. Remember that collection size alone is not the only factor. Age, quality, and appeal also factor into the equation.

Your automation software may be capable of generating reports for you that describes the age of the collection and the average age of titles in each of the Dewey classification numbers. Seek assistance from your software vendor in generating these reports. They can be very helpful in your collection evaluation.

Be sure to include both the plan to discard old materials and the plan to acquire the desired new materials into your long-range or strategic plan. You will probably need to sell the weeding process to the librarians. The best way to do that is to involve them in the collection analysis and the collection development process from the beginning.

Once you have followed this process, write up the findings in a report and share it with the committee that assisted in developing it, as well as with your supervisors. Suggest that the librarians share it with their principals, parent support groups, school improvement teams, business partners, and other stakeholders.

Ordering, Purchasing Methods, and Cataloging

Ordering library materials is becoming easier and easier with online access to publishers' catalogs. Most of the large library materials vendors have Web sites from which librarians may directly order their books.

Purchasing

Your school district will have policies and procedures in place regarding purchasing methods. It is vital to follow those policies and procedures. There are several cautions:

- Caution librarians about ordering for preview—billing nightmares can follow
- Do not allow ordering without proper prior approval by supervisors
- Do not allow librarians to enter into contracts without prior approval
- Ensure staff follows board of education policy in all transactions
- Encourage staff to shop for the best buys and lowest shipping costs (unless district negotiated contracts prevent this)
- Consider processing costs when purchasing

Cataloging

Does your district plan to provide original cataloging for the materials or will the librarians purchase cataloging with the materials? There are pros and cons to each method.

Cataloging Your Own Materials

Pros	Cons
Accuracy	Cost of cataloging materials
Consistency	Amount of time spent per item
Tailor-made to fit your exiting collection	

Purchasing Pre-Cataloged Materials

Pros	Cons
No overhead expense	Inaccuracies
No staff devoted to cataloging	Inconsistencies
Time required processing the materials	Cost per item

Another difficulty in purchasing preprocessed materials is that some specialized materials such as upper level science and math materials, which are ordered from single or sole-source, small publishers or vendors, will not have the pre-cataloged option. Library staff will have to catalog these resources either at the central or local site.

Many school districts are now outsourcing or purchasing original cataloging for their materials. Carefully study the costs and benefits before you make your decision. Individual libraries and individual library systems tend to have their own unique ways of cataloging. The library system must decide how many separate records it will create for a title. Will each new edition get a new record? These factors must be considered when deciding about where cataloging will be done.

Processing Materials

Another big decision districts must make is whether to provide centralized processing or to leave each librarian and library on their own to process library materials. From a librarian's perspective, centralized library processing is nirvana. The benefits of central processing are many:

- Lower cost per item for processing
- Consistency and uniformity in processing
- Accuracy and consistency in cataloging
- More time for librarians to spend working with students

It is possible to place a "standing order" with a vendor for purchasing certain pre-processing components. Some vendors follow these standing orders fairly consistently while others routinely botch the processing orders. Ask the vendors about their capabilities.

Central Library Services

Districts that do have a central library media center typically have the some of following components and services:

Professional Library—A collection of books, journals, and media selected to support teachers, administrators, and other employees in the school district.

Acquisitions Department—A person or group of people who assist library media staff with selecting, ordering, and purchasing library supplies and materials.

Cataloging Department—A head cataloger and possibly support staff who do all of the original cataloging for the district school library media specialists.

Processing Staff—The people who perform all of the steps of processing the materials such as applying bar codes, spine labels, Mylar covers, and security tapes.

Copyright Clearinghouse—Staff who serve as a help desk or clearinghouse for questions from others across the school district regarding copyright.

Selection Guidance—Staff who pre-select materials for library media specialists to purchase for their individual schools.

Library Helpdesk—Staff who answer questions and assist librarians and library aides in working with library technology, the automated library management software, and online research databases.

Videocassette/DVD Library — A central lending library for media for the entire district.

Curriculum Assistance — Assistance with curriculum design for information literacy and technology, standards alignment, and long-range planning for libraries.

Staff Development — Professionals who plan and deliver in-service for district staff.

TV Programming Acquisitions — Staff who select and produce the instructional programming for the district channel, schedule the broadcasting, and duplicate video programming, where appropriate.

TV Broadcast/Production Studio — A studio with the capacity to broadcast instructional/promotional programming on an educational cable channel and/or produce original education or promotional programming in house.

Media Production Center — A center where teachers and other staff members may use die cut machines, laminators, photocopiers, bookbinders, and other types of production equipment.

Your district may be large and see these services as efficient and cost effective. Others may decide that due to the small size of the district, it does not need or cannot afford such a comprehensive service unit.

Weeding

Why must you encourage librarians to weed? It is their professional duty, but it is often something they will not do without your prompting and support. The collection in each of your libraries should be:

- Relevant
- Current
- Appealing
- Diverse
- Matched to the curriculum

When evaluating the collection in the area of science and social studies, pay particular attention to the areas of:

- Astronomy
- Geography
- Health and medicine
- Politics
- Technology
- World cultures
- Government
- Communication
- Transportation
- Engineering
- Education
- Earth sciences
- Paleontology

You must convince the library media specialists that the collection should fit the mission of their libraries, match the goals they have set for their collection development plans, and reflect their communities. This can be a tough marketing job for you. Again, involvement in the policy decisions can pave the way for the librarians' acceptance of the mission of weeding.

Studies show that weeding collections will increase circulation. It is your responsibility to ensure that library media specialists continue to weed. Weeding the old, obsolete materials creates the space for new materials. Weeding helps make the collection more current and it boosts circulation, thus encouraging students to read more.

Items to encourage librarians to consider for weeding are items that are:

- Mildewed, moldy
- Stained or torn pages
- Racist, sexist, or have poor quality illustrations
- Underused duplicates
- Non-circulated items
- Single titles by lesser-known writers
- Short story or story collections by lesser-known authors

Other considerations to make librarians aware of are the copyright date, the date last circulated, reading level, local interest, and enduring value. You may also wish to establish physical condition criteria for weeding worn out items such as:

- Books that have brittle, yellowing, or torn pages
- Books that have been marked in
- Books that have been mistreated
- Books with tattered covers
- Books that smell or are musty
- Books that have foxing (Rusty spots on the pages)

Weeding Cautions

Trained professional librarians should be the people who weed materials from a school library collection, not parents, volunteers, or teachers. It is sometimes very hard for teachers or parents to let go of an item, even though it is obsolete, out-dated, or poorly written. The non-professional sometimes sees a book as a book without critically evaluating its value to the collection. The best guidance you can give librarians is to not involve parents and teachers in the weeding process.

Trained professionals can spot racism, sexism, and stereotypical material when they see it. Even though a certain country no longer exists, the community volunteer might want to keep the book since it has such nice pictures. In fact, some people see it as a sacrilege to throw out a book. It can be very helpful to bring a team of expert weeders from your central office directly to the library media center to provide assistance to the library media specialists who need weeding help. A title such as *The Union of the Soviet Socialists Republic: The*

World's Largest Country may be as physically fresh as the day it was printed but it probably does not belong in a school library collection.

Weeding should be done over time, not in one fell swoop. It should be a slow and steady, annual process. Advise librarians to set a calendar or schedule for weeding the different sections of the collections and encourage the librarians to follow that schedule. Librarians need to clean and read the shelves as they weed. Your role is critical to the accomplishment of this routine task.

Before weeding items, you may ask librarians to confirm that the item is not on the Accelerated Reader™ list, in case another school uses that program. You may also wish to ask librarians to confirm that the title is not in *The Children's Catalog* or similar standard resources. Check on the Internet if they suspect a book might be a rare book. Try a site like the Antiquarian Book at <<www.abaa.org>>.

One method to use to help librarians make the decision about what to use is the MUSTIE method.

M Misleading information or factually inaccurate
U Ugly or worn-out
S Superseded or newer versions available
T Trivial or no literary merit
I Irrelevant to the needs and interests of the community
E Elsewhere, the information can be found some where else like the Internet or an encyclopedia

This method was devised as part of the CREW Method developed by the Texas State Library. For more information see <<http://www.tea.state.tx.us/technology/libraries/lib_downloads/weeding1.pdf>>.

If you confirm that your school board does not have a policy that governs the disposal of library materials, you will want to consider what you will ask the librarians to do with weeded library materials. If, indeed, you are free to decide that, the following is a list of ideas for disposing of weeded materials:

- Run a book sale for 10 cents or 25 cents
- Sell them at a second-hand bookstore
- Sell them on the Internet
- Donate them to a children's home or an abused women's shelter
- Donate them to immigrant shelters
- Find a recycler who will take them

Never allow library media staff to dump the discarded books in the school dumpster. The patrons find them and are deeply disturbed to see books thrown away.

Periodical Collection

Each librarian will probably want to select the periodical titles to purchase for his local library. The librarian will also decide how long the periodicals will be kept in the library. You, in your role of system supervisor, may become involved as budget and storage issues arise. You may wish to offer guidance on the portion of budget you advise being spent on periodicals, the length of time to keep them, and the methods used to store them. Figure 3.4, Library Budget Allotment, shows one way to allot a budget.

Figure 3.4

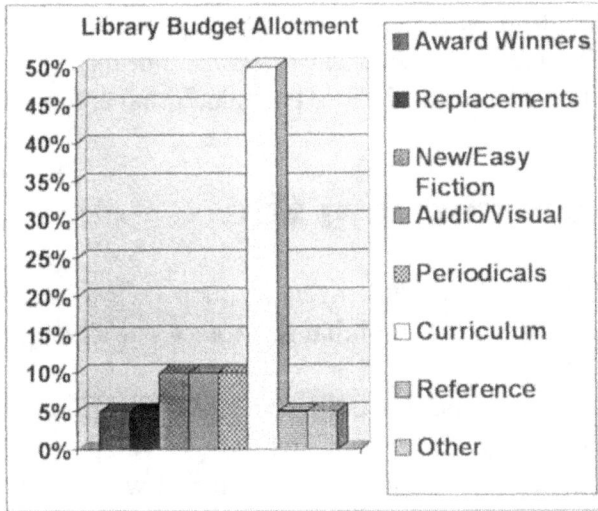

Censorship

The word "censorship" can send cold chills down the spine of a library media director. None of us wishes to be a censor. On the other hand, none of us wishes to intentionally offend our students and patrons. To avoid being placed in an unwanted position, select materials carefully. Your well-written, carefully thought-out, district materials selection policy will keep you safe. If the librarians in your district choose carefully, and if you have a solid and reasonable process to follow when objections occur about an item in your collection, you will weather the storm comfortably. The keys to success in avoiding censorship are:

- Adopt a reasonable selection policy.
- Get buy-in from the librarians, teachers, and administrators who will do the selecting.
- Ensure that librarians follow the selection policy.
- Adopt a well-thought-out objectionable materials policy.
- Get buy-in from all of the school district personnel, the school board, and the community on that policy.
- Follow your objectionable materials policy.
- Do not take knee-jerk actions just because you get a high profile objection.

Another part of avoiding censorship is to be flexible and use good sense. Most parents or community members who express a concern about library or instructional materials can be satisfied without entering a formal complaint system. It seems like the largest share of the complaints a district gets are from parents of younger students who wish to keep the student protected from the world as long as possible. The librarians need to work with the parents to help the child choose materials that are age-appropriate.

Should materials that are offensive because of stereotypical illustrations, biased perspectives, racist opinions, and other topics be included in your library school collections? If so, under what conditions should they be in the collection? If the teaching staff plans to teach a unit on Nazi Germany, they may need materials on that topic. Make sure that they have the right materials, not those from the biased views of cultures leftover from the 1950's that should have been weeded had the librarian been aware of them.

District Role for Inventorying the Collection

One of your responsibilities is to ensure that librarians inventory their collections. Your school district auditor or state statutes may determine how often you must make certain that librarians take inventory.

You may find it more cost effective to purchase the necessary electronic scanners for inventory and check them out to the school librarians. Develop a record-keeping system to keep track of which schools have inventoried which parts of their collection in which years.

Since inventory of a part of the collection is typically taken only once a year, you may also want to have designated staff at the central office who are familiar with the inventory software and hardware and who can assist the librarians in their once-a-year task. Encourage librarians to take inventory on parent conference days, teacher workdays, during final exam time, or other times where traffic is slower in the library. You may find that the school library inventory results are part of the data required on the principal's official state school report. Central library staff will need to develop written directions for librarians taking electronic inventory.

Library Automation System

Selecting a library automation system to purchase and install is another huge decision that a system of school libraries must make. When you are selecting a system, visit the districts and schools that have purchased the automated systems you are considering to see them in action. Some factors to consider when selecting a system are:

- Cost
- Versatility
- Ease of installation and conversion from current system
- Ease of use—intuitive navigational factors
- Options
- Compatibility with existing computer networks
- Hardware requirements
- Network requirements
- Long-term support from vendor

- Integration ability with other software
- Cost of upgrades

Once you have selected an automation system, you must convert existing data into the new system. Set aside plenty of time for training staff on the new system. Determine who will provide the training—you and your staff, or the vendor? Can the vendor provide a consultant for your district to train librarians and other key users? What will the cost of training and training materials be? Will those costs be included in the total cost of the system? Nail down those details before making final decisions.

When choosing an automation system, learn about the options for reports that the system offers. These reports can provide important information about your library system, so choose carefully. What do you absolutely need to know from the reports and what would you like to know, if possible?

The circulation system typically can tell you how your collection is circulating or not circulating by classification, interlibrary loan statistics, and the age of the collection. You will use these reports on an ongoing basis to help you with collection evaluation and development.

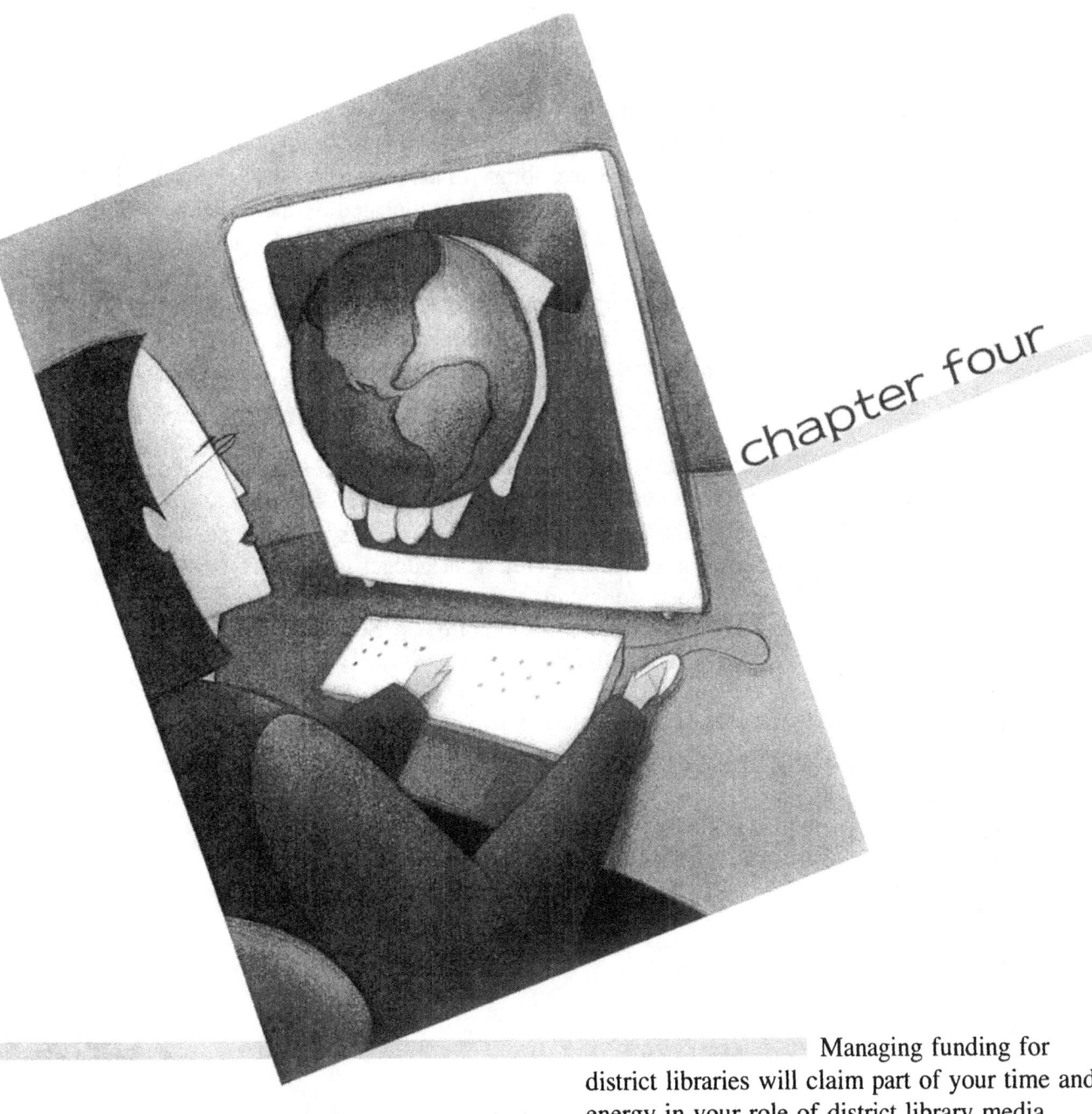

Budgets and Funding

chapter four

Managing funding for district libraries will claim part of your time and energy in your role of district library media director. Knowledge about needs assessment, as well as developing and understanding budgeting, is critical.

Operations Budget

Records show that the cost of library materials continues to rise. In many school districts, library budgets are being cut. These facts combine to create budget havoc for school libraries. In addition the need for up-to-date, accurate information for students and staff requires increased library funding. While advocating for more money for your libraries, you will also need to play the current funding hand you are dealt.

Methods for Budgeting

School districts typically distribute library funding in one of two ways. The district leadership either allocates the library funds directly to the school for site-based management, and the budget is, in turn, reallocated by the building principal; or the funding is under the control of the library media director to allocate to the school libraries.

As library media director, if you are asked to allocate the operations funding to the libraries in your system, you will need a method for distribution. You may have a system that is already in place and is working, or you may find the system needs a tune-up to provide greater equity for students.

Building Allocations Based on Size and Level

Some systems prefer to allocate the library budget money based on predetermined formulas for school population size and level. Elementary schools are categorized as small, medium, and large and are given a set budget for each of these three categories. Middle schools, if they are close in size of population, might be given one allocation and high schools another. Figure 4.1, School Library Allocations, may give you an idea of a way to allot funds.

Figure 4.1

School Library Allocations

The following are the school library budgets:

Elementary Schools
Small (250-399)	$6,000
Medium (400-599)	$7,000
Large (600-up)	$8,000

Middle Schools
Small (400-599)	$10,000
Medium (600-799)	$11,500
Large (800-up)	$13,000

High School $27,000

Another similar method is to determine a per-pupil allocation for students at each level: elementary, middle and high school. This method holds some advantages. The cost of materials per student at each level gets increasingly higher. There is greater equity in allocating an amount per pupil.

Because of efficiency of scale, you may find that you need to set a base amount for each school, and then allocate a per-pupil amount on top of the base allotment. This is necessary when you have both small schools and large schools. If you allocate on per-pupil alone, the small schools will not be able to afford to buy even the basics. Figure 4.2, Budget Per Pupil, offers another allocation example.

Figure 4.2

Budget per Pupil				
Elem School	2003-04 Population	$ per Pupil	Base Budget	03-04 Budget
School A	360	4.47	4675	6284
School B	310	4.47	4675	6061
School C	504	4.47	4675	6928
TOTAL	1174			$19,273
Middle School				
School A	625	5.10	8037	11225
School B	607	5.10	8037	11133
School C	526	5.10	8037	10720
TOTAL	1758			$33,077
High School				
School A	1881	4.13	19549	27318
School B	1971	4.13	19550	27690
School C	1919	4.13	19549	27474

Site-Based Budgeting

If your district is committed to site-based budgeting, you will have little or no control over how the building principals allocate funding to their libraries. You will have to be a tireless advocate for your libraries and work persuasively with building administrators. If your district budgets in this manner, connecting with building principals should be at the top of your professional goals. Regular visits to the schools are one way to establish a presence and develop a relationship with the building principals. Remember, you catch more flies with honey than you do with vinegar.

Capital Budget

Capital budgets are intended for purchasing the capital equipment that is necessary for your library system. All furniture, equipment, and technology are purchased from the capital outlay budget. Your long-range plan should help you as you determine what capital expenditures you will need to make in the future.

Furniture, shelving, security systems, circulation desks, and all types of equipment for the libraries will be purchased from your capital budget. You may also find that technology hardware is part of the capital equipment budget, if it is not in a separate technology budget. This makes it imperative to work closely with the technology director. As you request capital equipment, you will need to dust off your crystal ball and look into the future. What will you need next year in your libraries? What will you need in five and ten years? In order to answer these questions, you can conduct a simple needs assessment on your libraries.

Plan to keep careful records of your capital expenditures. Develop a matrix or tracking system to record the purchase and installation of library equipment at each library media center. This matrix will help you plan your capital equipment/furniture budget requests.

Depending upon the way you write your furniture specifications, which will be discussed in *Chapter 5*, you can predict the life of your library furniture. You can request furniture with lower standards and expect to replace it in a shorter time frame, or you can write higher standards and expect longer life expectancies for your furniture. With equipment and technology, obsolescence can be a greater factor than quality.

Fundraising Initiatives

It is a sad fact in today's world, but fundraising can be a part of the job of the library media director. Try to picture yourself as a philanthropic fundraiser; it could easily be part of your job. Below are some fundraising methods to consider if your assignment is to raise money for your libraries.

Business Partners—Many schools and school districts have established business partners. Each school has an opportunity to build a partnership with a neighboring business or a business with which staff or parents have a connection. For example, a local medical center that typically spends $10,000 for entertainment for their annual staff dinner might be willing to work with your school district. Could your high school choirs, jazz bands or theatrical groups provide the entertainment for that corporate staff dinner in exchange for a donation for your school libraries? It could happen and it could be a windfall for your library.

Friends of the Library—Many libraries find establishing friends of library groups a very beneficial endeavor. Frequently the friends of the library organizations collect used books and hold annual book sales to raise funds for the libraries. Some school librarians offer parents an opportunity to join the friends of the library organization on fee payment day. They offer the chance to participate at a variety of levels, just like your local public television station.

Corporate Sponsors—Some school districts live in an area that has a major business or industry. That entity may be interested in establishing a sponsorship in order to become involved in the community and to influence the quality of graduates the school system is sending into the workforce. Contact the corporate headquarters to begin to establish a relationship.

School Support Groups—Booster Clubs, parent teacher organizations, or student councils may be interested in supporting your libraries with volunteers, funds, and/or advocacy support. These booster clubs can help you with special projects.

Fundraisers—Cappuccino day, car washes, and other bake sale-type activities can raise funds for your libraries. They take go-getter volunteer organizers and plenty of effort. They can bring attention to the funding plight of your libraries as another benefit to your system. With the assistance of plenty of parent volunteers, a high school can hold a monthly cappuccino day in the library. They can sell coffee, hot chocolate, smoothies, and cookies. The students and staff would love the events and they could raise surprising revenues.

See Appendix D for an example of a flier requesting help from the community for librarians.

As you take your fundraising efforts on the road, you will need a set of facts or a district profile to show to potential funders. Figure 4.3, Media Services Profile, is a sample of one that might get you started thinking about one that would work for you.

Figure 4.3

SHAWNEE MISSION SCHOOL DISTRICT

Cynthia Anderson
Associate Superintendent for
Educational Services

Media Services Profile

Quality Libraries
- A quality library is open and staffed by an expert librarian in each school in our district. Our online collection contains more than one million (1,000,000) books and related materials.

Summer Libraries
- Several of our school libraries are open in the summer to provide quality reading material and innovative programming and instruction to our clients year-round.

Information Literacy
- Students can research topics online; browse electronic journals, encyclopedia, magazines and indexes; and access information from other libraries.

Award-Winning Library Staff
- Our 55 librarians devote their time and efforts to the task of improving all aspects of the library program. Several committees meet regularly to make recommendations regarding programs, technology and professional development.

Ancillary Staff
- Educational assistants and volunteers assist our professional librarians in many schools.

Title Library Connections
- Title I librarians meet monthly to learn reading strategies that can be implemented during student's library time.

Literature Appreciation
- Librarians foster life-long literacy and the appreciation of good books.

Media Services provides:

- *Central Library Processing for all library materials*
- *A Media Library of 5,000 videos and DVD titles to supplement curricula*
- *A Professional Library for the use of Shawnee Mission staff*
- *Library Acquisitions assistance for district librarians with selection resources, budget management, and materials acquisition*
- *Instructional Television programming for classroom teachers and students*
- *Assistance with copyright questions and other staff research needs*

2002-2003 Annual Circulation Averages

Schools	Totals
High School	62,980
Middle School	72,283
Elementary	1,059,307
School Totals District-Wide	1,194,570
District Media Centers	7,124
Total	1,201,694

Per Pupil Expenditures

Avg. per pupil library expenditure in SM 2001-02	$14.13
Avg. per pupil library expenditure nationally in 2001-02	$16.50
Avg. pupil library expenditure in SM in 2002-03	$4.37

Average Cost of Library Books 2002-03

Elementary	$20.00
Middle School	$27.00
High School	$35.00

Chapter Four: Budgets and Funding

Local Foundations

A trend across the country is for community leaders to establish foundations that are designed to support local school initiatives. You can find links to examples of these foundations on many school district Web pages. See the Blue Valley Educational Foundation's Web page at <<http://www.bvef.bluevalleyk12.org>> for one example.

Fines

Charging fines can be a revenue source for your libraries. Typically, elementary school libraries do not charge fines. More often, secondary school libraries charge fines. You and your administrators and librarians will need to determine your philosophical perspective on charging students fines for late materials. Some districts go so far as to withhold grade cards and transcripts until library fines are paid. Before setting a policy like that, you would need to check with district administrators to determine students' legal rights. This is another topic your library advisory committee might wish to tackle. Charging fines can be a bookkeeping nightmare and can generate very little funding at five cents a fine. It can also be a negative public relations plan.

Grants

Grant funds are available for school libraries. Getting those grant funds should be a goal for you and your school district. There are many grant funds available, even in today's economy. The art is to find the funding that matches your needs and then find the time and energy to write the grants. As the leader of your system of libraries, you will need to inspire yourself to head the grant writing effort and make it a priority.

There are several steps to getting grant funds:

Identify the Need—Determine what you need grant funds for. Provide supporting data, such as age of collection. When you describe the need, write it in a compelling and persuasive way.

Start Small—Cut your grant-writing teeth by finding some local funding first. Land a small grant before seeking large federal grants. Funders consider your past success in writing and overseeing grants, so get experience locally before going for the big money.

Locate the Grant Resources—Search until you find funders who are a match for projects for which you need funding. The Internet is a diamond mine of grant funds. Your job is to find them.

Attend Workshops or Seminars—Take a class or attend a seminar on grant writing to help you learn the ropes of grant writing. It will build your confidence and skills.

Collaborate—You increase your chances of getting grant funding when you collaborate with other entities such as a public library, an institution of higher learning, or another school. Funders prefer reaching as many students as possible when selecting projects to fund.

Assemble a Grant Writing Team—You will need to put together a team to help get the grant written. Divide the job of writing the grant into smaller parts, get several people working together, and you will make an easier time of the job of writing the grant.

Study the Selected Proposal/Application—Read and study the application carefully in order to comply with all of the guidelines. Read it with a highlighter in hand and highlight pertinent information. Read the request for proposal (RFP) again and again.

Gather Data and Make a Plan to Apply—Outline your plan for your grant request and then fill in the details. Do the research to make your proposal accurate and compelling.

Assign the Grant Writing Tasks and Set Deadlines—Working with your team, divide up the work and set deadlines that are sure to get the project done on time.

Oversee the Deadlines and Keep the Project Moving—Check in frequently with the grant writing team members and cheer them on in their work. Facilitate the process where necessary.

Ensure Accurate Editing and Proofreading—Pay close attention to details, edit the grant down to the bare essence, and proofread it again and again. Get help polishing your proposal.

Gain All of the Necessary Approvals—Get approval from your supervisor before you even start to write the grant. Once you have that approval and the grant is written, take the completed grant back for final approval before submitting it. You will need the approval of the superintendent, the business office, possibly the board of education, and certainly your boss before submitting the grant proposal.

For more detailed help in writing grants, check out a copy of the 2002 Linworth publication, *Write Grants, Get Money*. This book will walk you through the grant writing process, step by step. Grant funds are out there just waiting to be tapped. Do not let the task of writing a grant keep you from getting some of that money for your libraries. Some samples of grant funding available are:

- **Educational Technology State Grants**
  This Title II-D grant program is offered to improve student academic achievement through the use of technology in elementary and secondary schools. Districts are required to spend twenty-five percent of the funds they receive on professional development. To learn more, go to <<www.ed.gov>>.

- **Improving Literacy Through School Libraries**
  This Title I-B4 grant is designed to improve literacy skills and academic achievement by providing students with increased access to up-to-date library materials, well-equipped, technologically advanced, school library media centers; and well-trained, professionally certified school library media specialists. School districts with a child-poverty rate of at least 20 percent may apply directly to the U.S. Department of Education.
  In order to tap these federal funds from the reauthorization of the *Elementary and Secondary Education Act, No Child Left Behind*, you would need to analyze the age of the collection and decide which areas are most in need of

replacement. Another factor you will need to report is the length of time since your libraries have received funding. Funding can be used to acquire updated materials and technology, build connectivity, provide professional development related to early childhood literacy, and provide extended hours for students in your school libraries. To learn more about these grant funds, go to <<www.ed.gov/offices/OCFO/grants/forecast.html>>.

- **Laura Bush Foundation for America's Libraries**
  Find information about applying for $5,000 of funding at the following web site <<http://www.laurabushfoundation.org/>>. Grants from the Laura Bush Foundation are made to school libraries across the country to use to purchase books. Preference is given to schools in which ninety percent or more of the students qualify for free or reduced lunch.

- **LSTA Funding**
  Library Services Technology Act (LSTA) funds leadership and block grants that go to the states for set asides for state projects. The purpose of LSTA is to consolidate federal library services in all types of libraries to best serve the people of America. The specific federal LSTA goals are:

    1. Establish or enhance electronic linkages among or between libraries
    2. Electronically link libraries with educational, social or information services
    3. Assist libraries in accessing information
    4. Encourage libraries in different areas, and different types of libraries, to establish consortia and share resource
    5. Pay for libraries to acquire or share computer systems and telecommunications technologies
    6. Target library and information services to persons having difficulty using a library, and to underserved urban and rural communities.

- **Institute for Library and Information Literacy Education (ILILE)**
  This national competitive research grant opportunity is offered through Kent State University, Kent, Ohio. They have grants available for research projects that enhance teacher and librarian collaboration. To learn more, logon to <<www.ilile.org>>.

- **Reading is Fundamental (RIF)**
  Several funding opportunities are available from this foundation. Visit their Web site at <<www.rif.org>> for information.

- **American Association of School Librarian's Highsmith Research Grant**
  These two entities have collaborated to offer funding for action research in school libraries. Find more information at <<www.ala.org>> click on Awards/Scholarships.

- **Impact Aid**
  This federal grant program helps school district located near federal lands that may not be subject to property tax. Some of this money is awarded as basic support, which includes books and supplies. For more information, logon to <<www.ed.gov/offices/OESE/ImpactAid>>.

- **Innovative Programs**
  These grants are designed to help "promising educational reform programs and school improvement programs based on scientifically based research." Instructional and media materials are among the specifically identified funding priorities. Find help at <<www.ed.gov/offices/OESE/SST/ieps.htmls>>.

- **Barbara Bush Foundation for Family Literacy**
  This foundation provides grants of up to $65,000 for programs that combine literacy or pre-literacy instruction for children with literacy instruction for primary caregivers. Their Web site is <<www.barbarabushfoundation.com/nga.html>>.

- **The Starbucks Foundation**
  The foundation makes grants to programs that support its "Power of Literacy" initiative. Locate information at <<www.starbucks.com/aboutus/grantinfo.asp>>.

It pays to constantly be on the lookout for grant funds. Try these Web sites for more information.

GrantsAlert
GrantsAlert is a Web site that helps non-profits, especially those involved in education, secure the funds they need to continue their important work. They have information at <<http://www.grantsalert.com/>>.

Grant Writing Tips
SchoolGrants has compiled an excellent set of grant writing tips for those that need help in developing grant proposals. Try <<http://www.schoolgrants.org/grant_tips.htm>> for tips.

School Grants
A collection of resources and tips to help K-12 education apply for and obtain special grants for a variety of projects. Find them at <<http://www.schoolgrants.org>>.

U.S. Department of Education Grants and Contacts
This is a comprehensive list of all the U.S. Department of Education's active programs, including the Enhancing Education Through Technology Program. The database is searchable by topical heading, subject, education level, who may apply and other criteria. Log on to <<www.ed.gov/funding.html>>.

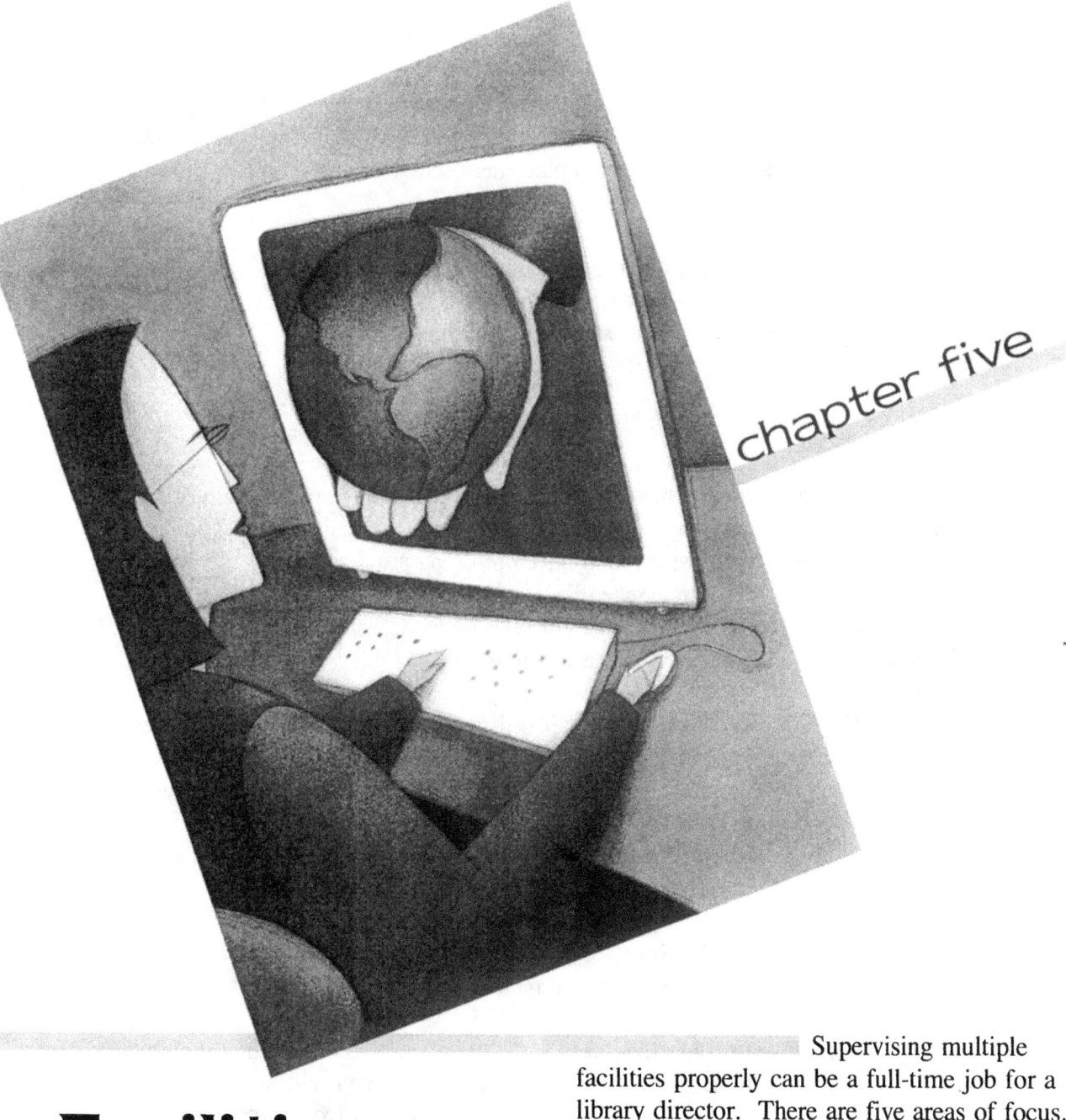

Facilities

Supervising multiple facilities properly can be a full-time job for a library director. There are five areas of focus.

- Maintaining existing facilities
- Planning for new and remodeled libraries
- Moving and/or closing libraries
- Planning to avoid disasters
- Disaster recovery

Maintaining Existing Facilities

Depending upon your particular situation and the size of your school district, you may have a direct role in ensuring regular maintenance of library facilities. If so, no matter how many facilities you oversee, you will need a plan to keep them well maintained. Keeping good records and making a maintenance schedule can help you. Areas to consider placing on a routine maintenance/replacement schedule are:

- Painting
- Carpet or flooring replacement
- Blind or window covering replacement
- Furniture and/or shelving replacement
- HVAC

Paint

Your school district or library system may have a maintenance schedule which includes interior repainting. If not, you will need to assess the condition of each of the libraries in your system and develop a repainting schedule. Seven to ten years is a typical repainting schedule.

When repainting, you must consider how extensive the repainting must be. What areas will be included in the repainting cycle?

Walls   Will you repaint all walls or only those near the entrances, exits, circulation desk, and other high traffic areas? If your perimeter shelving does not have backs on them, you will need to remove all of the books on the perimeter shelves in order to reach the walls. If you decide this is necessary, you will need to make arrangements to:
1. Remove the library materials
2. Relocate the materials to a safe storage location
3. Replace the materials back on the shelves

Ceilings   In some facilities you may encounter ceilings that require repainting. In those circumstances you will need to make arrangements to protect the collection from exposure to paint drips from the ceiling during the repainting.

Carpet

When carpet or flooring needs replacement, you face many of the same issues as you do when repainting. Will all or only part of the collection need to be relocated for the re-carpeting?

Blind or Window Covering

This renovation should interfere less with your library functioning than repainting or recarpeting. Look for ease of maintenance, cost of materials, installation costs, durability, energy conservation, and function as you choose window coverings. How dark do you need your library to be? What issues do you have with glare or heat that need to be solved with the new window treatments? Be sure to consider these factors when choosing window coverings.

Furniture and/or Shelving Replacement
Replacing furniture or shelving can be a major purchase and requires a great deal of planning and effort. There are many decisions you must make. Will you have wooden or metal shelving? Do you want backs in your shelving or open-backed? Do you want the shelves to be held in place in the bookcase with a pegs and holes, or a strips and clips system? Do you want to keep the same configuration of furniture and shelving placement or are you planning on redesigning the floor plan of your library? Also decide if you want adjustable or fixed shelving, double- or single-faced. Remember to accommodate ADA compliance for aisles and shelving heights.

Rearranging Furniture
Sometimes you just need to rearrange the existing furniture in a library in order to get a more efficient floor plan or to better utilize the space. When that is necessary, draw a floor plan to scale, make scale cutouts of the existing furniture and then rearrange on paper until you, the librarians and the building principal are satisfied with the plan. Once you have agreement, call for help from your operations and maintenance department to rearrange your space.

Later in this chapter we will look at writing furniture specifications and working with furniture vendors. We will also look at some of the pros and cons of the different types of library furniture. Be sure to keep careful records of the furniture replacement cycle for your libraries.

Planning for New or Renovated Libraries
Making long-range facility plans can be a complex process. A needs assessment should be conducted. Factors to analyze are:

- Population growth or decline in the school
- Current condition of the new facility
- Maintenance history and current schedule
- Budget prospects now and in the future
- Potential changes in use

When you are planning to build a new library or planning a major remodel of an existing facility, you will need to work with a team of architects and school system staff. Ideally you will include representatives from all stakeholders as you begin planning. Your librarian, superintendent, building administrator, technology director, and district facilities manager should all be considered for the planning team.

Selecting and Working With the Architects
Some school districts have a process for screening architectural firms before selecting the project architect. Lobby to be on the selection team, if your district uses a committee or team.

When selecting an architectural firm, first check their past experiences and references. Not all architects have designed successful school libraries. Hire a firm that has had laudable experience in this field. It is advisable to meet with several firms and let them pitch their designs to you before making the final choice of design firms. Ask for references from libraries and be sure to contact the library directors. If the architectural firm has someone who specializes in libraries on staff, arrange to meet with that person.

As you meet and plan your new library, expect a cast of many at your meetings. Between the staff from your district that you bring to the planning table, combined with the design team of architects, electrical engineers, mechanical engineers, and interior designers the planning meetings may be large and frequent.

Communicate regularly throughout the project with your design firm. Ask your superintendent to be included on the project oversight team that oversees the project. Meet frequently, check for understanding and monitor closely.

You will need to compromise throughout the process. Everything will not go your way. Expect to practice the art of compromise with grace. The budget may be tight and sacrifices may need to be made, so be prepared to bend a little.

Field Trips

Plan and take field trips with your team. Visit other libraries, both new and older ones, with your team and try to build consensus on the qualities you want to include in your library. State your preferences up front with the design firm. Make a careful list of your "must haves," "like to haves," and "do not want to haves." Be sure that you have these preferences in writing and that you discuss them with the architect. See Appendix E for a sample document.

Beginning to Plan

Design Phase

During the design phase, you will need to make a final plan for the use of the space and the placement of the shelving, equipment, computers and furniture. Pay special attention to the arrangement of space. How many classes do you need to accommodate in the library at once? Try to design a space for two complete classes in each elementary library and a space for three classes in each secondary library. The library is typically the meeting place of the school so you would need seating for the entire staff, if that is where staff meetings are held.

When looking at the general layout, where will the stacks be located? Where will classes be held? Where will you place the reference section? Again, find a way to establish ideal supervision from all areas as you plan. What will the size of your library be? No matter the actual size, try to create a sense of space. Give the eye space to glide. Avoid chopping up your space and creating visual disharmony. Study public spaces whose sense of space you admire and try to replicate that. Tailor your lighting plan to the use of the space. Make sure you are making accommodations for technology.

Be flexible. It may be more efficient to put in more computer drops now than you have computers in order to expand services later. Try to consider future uses and needs.

Attend to the Details
You will be working with experts on these details but you will need to pour over the plans with careful attention. Where will strategic power and data connections be located in the new facility? How much capacity should you build in? There is the potential for many errors as you plan so pay careful attention. The quote "God is in the details," is often attributed to Bauhaus architect Mies van der Rohe. Although the attribution of the quote is unverifiable, the sentiment it expresses is absolutely true.

How high will your perimeter shelving be? Will the emergency strobes, fire alarms, and light switches be located in a spot where you plan to have 72" or 84" wall shelving? If so, work with the engineers to find a way to meet code and maximize your wall space storage. It can be done. Chances are that the electrical engineers will be nowhere to be found when the shelving installers give you the bad news that the emergency strobe lights prohibit the installation of the last section of shelving. As you plan, pay close attention to the blueprints and check carefully to ensure the proper location and capacity of the following:

- Power
- Data
- Fire alarms
- Strobes
- Light switches
- Public address systems
- Clocks

For up-to-date, comprehensive help on interpreting blueprint symbols do an Internet search on blueprint symbols. There are several helpful sites.

Make many and frequent site visits during the construction phase to avoid big problems later. Make careful notes of the location of the strategic things that have been discussed. Take your digital camera with you and print out the pictures when you return to your office.

Lighting the Stacks
Proper lighting is essential to a successful library design. Watch carefully when you visit other libraries and note the attributes of successful lighting installation. Things to consider:

- Run lighting parallel to the stacks
- Check the lighting standards
- Use Mother Nature when you can

Accent Lighting
You can make a dramatic emphasis in special areas of your library with accent lighting. Consider your needs and desires before meeting with the architects.

Task Lighting
Do you need desk lamps in your study areas? Will you purchase lighted study carrels? If so, plan ahead for power needs.

Clerestory Lighting and Sky Lights
Many architects like to include clerestory lighting in libraries. There are both benefits and cautions for this type of lighting. This can provide natural light but also can provide a bad glare. To avoid glare, predict where the sun will be at each period of the day. Will it enhance learning or provide glare for the learners? You also need to consider multimedia use. Don't forget that you will need areas of the library which can be darkened for viewing multimedia presentations. Locate the light switches or dimmers in a place handy to the teacher/librarian.

Classroom Lighting
Plan ahead to provide adequate and flexible lighting for the classroom areas of your library. Provide a way to keep your stacks lighted while you darken other areas of your library for multimedia presentations. Plan to use zoned lighting. Again, where will the control switches for the lighting be located in order to be most convenient for staff and students?

Natural Light and Windows
Let nature provide you with energy efficient, inexpensive natural light when and where you can. Look out and plan for:

- Avoiding glare
- Addressing solar heating issues
- Purchasing blinds or shades
- Considering sky lights that make adequate night time lighting difficult

If you have interior windows from one room of the library to another, place interior windows at a height of 42" above the floor. That will allow you to place 42" shelving under the windows and it will also allow you to see through the window for supervision even when seated at a desk or table. Beware of interior windows that go to the floor. They do not allow any shelving under the windows on either side. They often reveal clutter on the other side of the window as well as take up valuable wall space that could be used for shelving.

Always consider glare when designing windows in your new or remodeled library. Provide a vista when you can. When possible, place your windows toward tranquility, a view, a garden or an oasis. Try to avoid providing a view of the school loading dock or trash dumpster.

Acoustics
Young people who are actively learning produce noise. Think ahead with your design team to make conditions ideal. Watch carefully for good acoustics in the classroom area(s) of your library.

Technology

It is possible that new technology will be designed and produced between the time you plan your new library and the time it is built. Do your best to look to the future as you plan and build capacity for change into your design. You can always purchase new equipment in the future. Make sure you have designed your library to use more equipment than you currently own. Put in more computer and data drops than you think you will need.

Shelving Your Collection

You must determine both the current size of your collection as well as the possible future size when planning shelving. If you are starting a brand new library, predict your future ideal collection size and plan now to accommodate that. What are your holdings? As you estimate your needs, count 30 books per shelf. Take a careful inventory before the design process begins and also count the number of shelves of books and other materials that you currently have. The calculations for shelving needs for a new library are represented in Figure 5.1 (on next page), Calculating Necessary Shelving.

Try to design the library to maximize wall space for shelving in order to maximize floor space for people and programs. There is nothing as fine as wide-open spaces in a library. You must also consider supervision. Where will the library staff be spending most of their time? Where might supervision blind spots be? Will you have a stacks area? Can you see down each aisle from all areas? Consider supervision from all angles and make sure the aisles widths meet ADA standards.

Signage is another consideration. Will you purchase signage from library providers or will the architectural team be developing signage? Have you planned in your budget for signage?

Selecting a Color Scheme

If you are working with a design team, your design team will work with you as you design the interior color scheme. Again, take digital pictures and make notes when you visit other libraries. Study effective color schemes in public spaces. Aim for soothing, calming color pallets for your patrons. Try to:

- Avoid trends
- Avoid cute
- Think of the future
- Use neutrals to calm your guests
- Put "brights" in smaller areas where they can be changed
- Avoid trendy colors in high elevations that are difficult to reach to repaint

Providing for Special Needs

Plan your space for all types of users. Make the space accessible to those in wheelchairs and to those with special technology needs. Provide signage in Braille. Do your best to design an inclusive space and make sure all ADA

Figure 5.1

Calculating Necessary Shelving

1. Determine current collection size (holdings) in:
    - Books
    - Videos
    - CD's
    - DVD
    - Other media

2. Estimate potential collection size you may have once you are in the new or remodeled facility.

3. Estimate the number of shelves needed by using 30 books per shelf for:
    Fiction
    Easy
    Each Dewey classification

    20 books per shelf for:
    Reference materials

4. Examine the floor plan drawing or blueprint and determine where the different heights of shelving can be placed:
    42"
    60"
    72"
    84"

    Count for each 36" wide section of shelving:
    42" high – 3 shelves
    60" high – 5 shelves
    72" high – 6 shelves
    84" high – 7 shelves

5. Multiply 30 books times the number of shelves you plan to purchase to get a total capacity for the new library.

6. Determine if the shelving unit will be single-sided wall shelving or double-sided, free-standing.

    Double the shelving capacity when calculating double-sided free-standing shelving.

7. Plot how you will shelve your collection on each wall and on the free-standing shelving units.

8. Determine where each section (100's, 200's, etc.) of the book collection will be shelved and confirm that there is adequate shelving.

9. Using your collection size of each type of media, and the capacity of each unit of media storage, determine the type and number of media storage units you will need.

10. Shelving depth varies. While 10" deep shelving will accommodate most fiction collections, 12" deep shelving is preferable for non-fiction, picture books and reference. Videos can be shelved on eight inch deep shelving.

11. Ask yourself:
    - How many shelves of picture books do I currently have?
    - How many shelves of fiction do I have?
    - How many shelves of non-fiction do I have?
    - How many shelves of reference books do I have?
    - How many shelves, drawers, etc. of media do I have?

    Make sure you can accommodate your collection in the new facility.

12. Do not forget to include any special collections you have.

requirements are met. For detailed guidelines, go to the U.S. Department of Education Web site at www.ed.gov. More information is available in Janet Hopkins' book *Assistive Technology: An Introductory Guide*.

Considering Supervision

Plan your library with the objective of good supervision built into it. Make sure there aren't nooks and crannies where trouble can erupt unseen by the staff. Theft, monkey-business, and safety issues can occur when the facility has spots that cannot be easily observed.

Planning for Furniture and Selecting the Furniture

Will you need new furniture in your new or remodeled facility or will you be using the old? Either way, you will need a carefully drawn-to-scale floor plan on which to locate your scale drawings of furniture. Make yourself some photocopies of the scale furniture. Use replaceable double stick tape on your scale furniture drawings so that you may try your furniture placement in a myriad of ways before deciding on your final plan.

When choosing upholstered furniture like sofas, lounge chairs and chair seats, be sure to consider durability, comfort, cost, use, maintenance, and esthetic qualities. Remember, in elementary schools, lice can make themselves at home in upholstered furniture that touches heads.

When selecting furniture there are many items to consider. Budget, durability and intended use are some of them. Contact several vendors and ask about their products and suggestions. When choosing chairs, benches, and stools, some choices you must make are:

- Wood or upholstery
- Sled or leg base
- Seat height and width
- Task chairs' style and use

Picture Book Shelving

Consider your need for shelving designed specifically for picture books. Do you need it? Can you afford it? One caution: consider the height of your young children as you order picture book shelving. Three-shelf-high units are about as tall as your patrons can reach. What types of signage will you need for picture books? What types of display furniture will you need for your young readers? You will want to use double-sided shelving for your free-standing picture book shelving.

Tables

Think about how many classes you plan to seat in the library and what other purposes you plan for your tables. Refer back to the picture file you made of other libraries. Consider the shapes, sizes, number and types of table furniture you will need and make some decisions.

Writing Furniture Specifications

You are fortunate indeed if you already have written specifications for bid purposes for library furniture. If you do not already have them, you will need to:

- Consider needs
- Check the standards
- Take field trips
- Look at samples
- Network with others
- Consider budget and life expectancy
- Set priorities
- Write specifications

See Appendix F for a sample of furniture specifications. After you have written your furniture specifications, be sure to carefully scrutinize them. It is vitally important that you check them with a fine-toothed comb. What you put on the bid proposal is what you will get, nothing more. If there are errors, now is the time to find them and fix them.

Confirm that you have calculated the correct number of starters and adders for all your shelving and that each set is the correct height. Check measurements once more to make sure that what you are buying will fit into your space. Corrections can be made easily now, but not later when the furniture has been built, shipped, and installed.

Make sure that your furniture is not blocking fire extinguishers, alarms, pediment, windows, doors, and drinking fountains.

Areas to Include in the New or Renovated Library

Classroom Area

Every school library must have a classroom. Most need two classroom areas and some need three. Considerations are:

- *Number of Students*—How many users will you have in each class? 24-28?
- *Number of Classes*—Allow for one, two, three or even four in some large high schools.
- *Multimedia Presentation Equipment*—Can it be permanently installed? Where will the screens be? Can they be automated? Do you have control of lighting in that location?
- *Acoustics*—How many classes will be receiving instruction at once? How can you physically seclude them to improve acoustics? Watch out for vaulted ceilings in classroom instructional areas. They pose acoustical problems for teaching areas.
- *Distractions*—Try your best to place classroom instructional items areas away from major distractions like the circulation desk, water fountain, entrances and exits.

- *Space for Portable Computer Lab Cart Storage*—Allow for an area to park the mobile lab cart(s).

Circulation Desk

Many prefer the circulation desk centered in the library. Others prefer the circulation desk near the exit. Do your homework and decide what your preferences and needs are. Consider the following:

- *Location*—Centrally located or near an exit? What components will you need? Do you need open or closed storage or some of both?
- *Storage*—What will you be storing in this area? Will you need a book drop within the circulation desk? If so, which location is most convenient to the staff and patrons?
- *Computers/Printers*—Where within the desk will you need to place the computers and printers? How many will you need?
- *CPU On or Under the Desk*—Most people prefer to locate the CPU under the circulation desk. If so, plan for that as you design and order components.
- *Phones/Faxes*—Where, how many, and what kind of phones and faxes will you need?
- *Locked or No Lock*—Will you need secure storage? If so, for what? Be sure to specify where you want locked and no lock storage.
- *Demagnetizer Shelf*—Don't forget to place this security device in a convenient spot.
- *Display*—Will you need to display seasonal, new, or high interest materials at the circulation desk? Where will that display area be located?
- *Accessibility*—Be sure you meet all ADA codes and the needs of all your users when you plan the circulation desk. One section must be accessible at wheelchair height.
- *Purchase or Build*—Some architects prefer to design and build the circulation desk. Others are counting on you to purchase the circulation desk. Decide and agree on this important point during the design phase. Some tips:
    39" high secondary
    32" high elementary
    ADA requirements

Head-end Room/Tape/DVD Storage

Many secondary school libraries are designed with head-end tech rooms. Technology is mercurial in nature and requires you to do some forward thinking in order to build what you need for this year's program along with the capacity to run the systems of the future. What do you picture now in the multimedia area of the new library?

- Video distribution system
- Tape duplication capacity
- Tape storage
- Security for the equipment
- Satellite tuners
- Voice and data drops
- Building servers
- DVD burners
- Video juke box playout system
- Telephony equipment

Video Editing Equipment

Many directors want video editing bays in their new secondary school libraries. If so, work carefully with your design team to make sure you have all of the necessary power and data drops in the locations you will need them. If your district empowers and encourages students to produce videos, you may wish to explore building editing bays into your new facility. Another area to consider in your planning is an in-house TV studio for broadcasting and/or TV program production.

Story Area

A story area is *de rigueur* for an elementary library and something to consider in a secondary library that might serve teen-aged moms.

Some issues to consider are:

- Safe harbor for storytelling, puppet shows, and storytime
- Picture book shelving
- Reading table
- Rocking chair
- Display for stuffed animals
- Floor seating
- Big book storage and display

Periodicals

You may wish to incorporate a space for magazine and journal reading as well as storage in your new library. If so, as you make your plan, calculate the number of titles you wish to store and the period of time you wish to keep them. Accommodate a seating area next to the periodical displays.

Movable storage is one way to conserve floor space needed for periodical storage but plan installation carefully. While the initial installation cost is higher than traditional shelving, the space conservation is valuable to you. Vendors of this type of storage would be willing to work with you as you explore this option. They will draw you a scale drawing and help you picture the capacity of storage possibilities.

How do you plan to display periodicals in your new library? Are you using wall space for display or free standing furniture? Do you want wooden, Lucite, or metal storage units or do you want something dreamed up by the architect? Do your research as you visit other libraries. Look at their periodical reading areas and decide on the type of periodical storage that you prefer.

Reading Room

When designing the reading room, focus on:

- Supervision
- Durability
- Ambiance
- Comfort
- Lighting

Workroom

Every library needs a workroom for the library staff. Your workroom should include:

- A desk area for each librarian and library assistant
- A sink with running water to use when cleaning books and making coffee
- Computer/data, phone, and fax outlets
- Plenty of power outlets
- An area for secure storage of valuables

You should also have windows from the workroom to the library for supervision. Be sure that the librarian can still see out the windows of the workroom into the library, even when seated.

Professional Library

A secondary library is likely to include a professional library for teachers to use as a base from which to work during their planning times. Plan for:

- Windows for supervision from the professional library
- Phone, Internet access, data and cable TV drops
- Shelving
- Seating
- AV equipment for AV preview

Editing Bays

If you are planning video editing bays in your library, make sure they have:

- Voice and data drops
- Power outlets
- Supervision
- Videoconferencing/editing equipment
- Equipment purchase

Conference Rooms

The entire school community may use the library conference rooms at one time or another. When you're planning the conference rooms consider:

- Size and capacity
- Function
- Phone/data needs
- Number of conference rooms
- Furnishings and equipment for conference rooms

Computer Stations

You will need stations for online catalog use, Internet access, online reference database use, multimedia projects, and reference use. You may want both distributed stations and clustered stations. Distributed stations dispersed about the library be convenient to various purposes. Clustered stations will be convenient for assitance, instruction, and supervision. Decide how many of each type you need and where you will place them.

Computer Lab

Many people prefer to locate a computer lab within or adjacent to the library. If you need to plan for a computer lab some things to consider are:

- Ability to monitor and supervise
- Number of stations and printers
- Number of drops
- Entrances and exits
- Security of equipment

Art Gallery

Many high school libraries include an art gallery to feature students' work. This can range from a simple plan to display two-dimensional student art on the walls, to a more complex plan to provide a highlighted space for rotating art installations. Plan with your team and decide on your needs and preferences. Consider:

- Hanging art
- Display cases
- 3-dimensional art
- Security

TV Studio

This high-ticket item may or may not be part of the plan for your new library design. If it is to be part of your design, you will need to answer many technical questions before beginning the design process. Get professional help with decisions about:

- Production sets
- Switchers
- Satellite links
- Distance learning equipment
- Air shift desk
- Digital video playout system
- Broadcast equipment
- Lighting
- Sound

You will need this high-dollar space to be secure, so plan ahead for security features. Will you also need special temperature controls in the studio?

Storage Area
Will your new library need to include storage areas? If so, you will probably store:

- AV hardware
- AV software
- AV repair area
- Promotional materials

Security System
Plans for a new secondary library will probably need to include a security system at each entrance and exit. Assess whether your existing security system can be moved and reinstalled in the new library. If it cannot, can you modify it and add to it, or do you need a completely new system? Check with vendors, consider writing a grant proposal and be prepared to write bid specifications. Be sure the design team plans for power needs and is aware of restrictions in the security systems area such as no metal studs within so many feet.

Water and Restrooms
Do you want to include restrooms and a drinking fountain within your library complex? Will you need a sink in your library workroom? Plan for them now to avoid disappointment later.

Moving, Relocating, and Closing Libraries

Preparing to Move
If you are planning to move out of an existing facility and either move back in later or move to a new facility, there is no sense in moving, storing and reinstalling items that should have been discarded. Make sure you do an extensive evaluation of the collection before packing day. Weed, weed, and weed some more. If an item is outdated, inaccurate or inappropriate, discard it. Do not take obsolete materials, equipment, or furniture with you to the new library. Be sure to follow state law and your district policies on the disposal of obsolete materials.

Relocating the Collection

Should you need to relocate your collection temporarily for repainting, re-carpeting, or remodeling, you will need a thorough plan. Points to consider when making a temporary relocation plan for your collection are:

Manpower—Who can remove the books from the shelves and replace them later? Can you use existing staff or will you need to hire temporary help? If you have no budget for this, will you need to find volunteers?

Equipment—What will you use on which to offload the books and other materials? Book trucks? Large wooden temporary storage carts? Cardboard boxes? Can you borrow them or must you rent them?

Labeling—You will need a careful system for labeling in order to remove the collection and store it temporarily in order to reshelve it in the correct order. The proper labeling of your collection as you store it will make for a smooth reinstallation later.

Floor Plan Drawing—You will need a careful drawing or floor plan which is coordinated with your labeling system to ensure that the materials are reshelved in the proper order in the correct location. All of the key players in the removal and reinstallation will need copies of this plan.

Storage Conditions—You will need to maintain appropriate conditions in your temporary storage locations. Consider temperature, light, humidity and security when you select the temporary storage location.

Technical Support

When you move out of your old library and into the new or newly remodeled one, you will need to call for technical support. You will need expert tech support for:

- Planning for the new library
- Taking down the technology in the old facility
- Storing the equipment
- Setting up the equipment in the new library
- Reconnecting the equipment and bringing your network back up

Installation of Furniture and Shelving

Once the planning and construction or remodeling is done, you will be ready to install your library furniture. The proper installation of the new equipment, technology, shelving, and furniture is another critical area for a successful opening of your new or remodeled library.

Keep a careful calendar of projected delivery dates and confirmed installation dates and constantly compare it to the anticipated completion dates. Follow construction carefully and adjust the delivery and installation dates when necessary. Keep in close contact with your furniture vendors when the furniture installers arrive. The delivery team and the installation team are often from two or more different organizations and sometimes even two different cities.

It is vital that the school staff be expecting the delivery of the library furniture when it arrives. Be sure to keep the school staff in the loop so they know to accept delivery and to contact you when furniture and equipment arrives.

Here are some tips for a smooth installation or reinstallation:

- Be there—Don't assume that the installation will be carefree and that you are not needed on site.
- Cheer them on—Bring donuts for the workers. Bring good cheer and positive strokes. Careful installers are worth rubies and pearls. Keep them on your side. Treat them with kindness. It will serve you well.
- Bring plenty of maps—Before the installation, make several photocopies of the floor plan showing furniture placement. Give one to every installer you meet. Post them on doorjambs and windows, all over the library.
- Measure carefully—Be there as shelving is placed on angles. Once the installation has begun, measure the angles of placement. Check the clearance measurements. Ensure that you are following ADA requirements. Now is the time to make adjustments, not after the materials are on the shelves.

Furniture Vendor Punch List

After the installation of your new shelving and furniture, develop an accurate punch list of corrections that need to be made and start to work with your vendors. Work with your boss and the business office to consider withholding full payment until all of the glitches have been ironed out and all of the missing components installed. Once the bill is paid, service and follow-through can deteriorate.

Rome Was Not Built in a Day

Do not let impatience get the best of you. Inevitably you will be waiting for one or two late-arriving pieces of furniture or equipment to complete your project. Tips:

- Be flexible
- Communicate
- Be a team player

Celebrate

Celebrate each phase of your project. Once your new library is designed and built, you are ready to have a groundbreaking ceremony.

Call the media, don your hard hats, invite the board members, and tie bows on your shovels. This is a terrific opportunity for some positive press for your new library.

Have a dedication once the library is complete. Be sure to invite the stakeholders, benefactors, friends of the library, and all who care about the new library.

Show off the new facility at an open house. Fill the tea urn, bake the cookies, invite your community, and show off your new library. Get your student council, student leadership team, and friends of the library involved as tour guides.

Invite the chamber group to play in the library. A new library is an asset for your community and a reason to celebrate.

One of the saddest jobs you can have as a library director is the job of closing an existing library. This can happen when your district has declining enrollment and a school must be closed. There are many responsibilities for the library director when required to close a school library.

- Timeline—You will need a careful timeline to plan your library closing. Start planning as soon as you know you will be closing a facility. Make a plan for when the following events will occur.
- Weeding—It is a sad but true fact that there are items in the closing library collection that should be weeded. The librarian will probably need your help with this project. Schedule some times to work with him; roll up your sleeves and assist with the weeding. Totally worn-out items need to be discarded along with obsolete, unused, dated, and otherwise no-longer-useful items. This is a good time to discard old filmstrips, disk recordings, Apple IIe software, and other oldies but goodies. Get a shelf list printed to assist in determining the age of the collection.

  You will need a team of workers to help you with the weeding procedure and the process of discarding the materials. This work needs to be done discretely since feelings may be sensitive at this time of pending school closing.
- Asset Reallocation—There are many assets in a school library and decisions must be made about how they will be reallocated. If the students and staff in the closing school are being reassigned to other neighboring schools, those receiving schools should be the first beneficiaries of the assets of the closing libraries. Any special collections that were donated by or in honor of students and staff should follow those students and staff to the new location.

Once the collection has been weeded, print out a new shelf list of the holdings of the closing library and have the receiving librarian study it to see which assets would best fit in the receiving library. Set a time for the receiving librarian to come to the closing facility and select the items that have been marked on the shelf list. You will also want the teachers in the closing school, who are moving to other schools, to indicate the resources that are critical to their particular units of study. Make sure the resources follow the teachers.

Once the receiving librarian has selected the items that fit in the receiving collection, make a plan for the other district librarians to choose items for their libraries. This event should take place as late as possible in the school closing cycle. If possible, it would be ideal to have this "open library-shopping event" once school is dismissed so that students and parents are not present. If this is not possible, hold the "open house" late in the day, after school is dismissed. Be sensitive of the feelings and emotions of the closing school's staff.

One distribution method is to prepare strips of paper with the other schools' names and school numbers on them. Provide these strips to the "shopping" librarians and ask them to place the strips in the books they are selecting to facilitate reprocessing to their libraries. Make sure you have made provisions for space for librarians to stack or box their selections to await reprocessing. Again, you will need a team of workers with you to accomplish this asset reallocation event and process.

Seek help from your technology team in order to convert the computers in the closing library. Get them to install the software you will need to use to convert the location data. Staff can then change the designated locations of the materials in the library management database to the new locations. Plan ahead for this access to your database.

You can use a similar system in order to reallocate the library furnishings. Be sure to assess the furniture and shelving, and reassign the major pieces to other libraries by working with the receiving librarians and principals. The items that you do not reassign can be open to reassignment as the librarians and administrators from other schools visit the asset reallocation event.

You will also need to plan with your district's moving team to move the reprocessed materials and furniture to the receiving libraries. The materials must be kept in cool, light, dry spaces while in temporary storage in order to avoid mold infestation or other damage.

Planning to Avoid Disasters

Another part of the job is to plan ahead to avoid facility disasters. Take a look at some preventative measures that can be taken.

- Insurance—Research the types of coverage you currently have and determine if it is adequate. Consult with your business office and supervisor to discuss your coverage.
- Fire—Smoke damage and fire and water damage from fighting the fire can devastate a library. Prevent fires and smoke damage by installing smoke detectors and a fire suppression system in your library.
- Water—Do what you can to locate your libraries outside known flood plains. Be involved when any roof work is planned so that you are ready to respond in case of leaks.
- Mold—Mold is devastating but can be prevented. When the carpets are shampooed, make sure that the dehumidifiers are running until the humidity level is where it should be. Leave the lights on when necessary. Keep the library air conditioned in the summer, even when it is not in use. Mold grows in dark, damp, humid, warm places, and it loves books.
- Data—Work with your information technology department and make sure that you have a plan to avoid the loss of your library data.

Disaster Emergency Response

Get a committee of stakeholders together and develop a response plan to potential disasters. Be ready for:

- Fire
- Water or flood damage
- Mold
- Power Outage
- Loss of computer system
- Loss or contamination of data

As you develop your plan, you will need to answer questions such as:

- If you must relocate temporarily, where will that be?
- How will you communicate during the event?
- Who will play which roles in the emergency plan?

Develop calling trees and phone lists of emergency numbers. Meet frequently with your team until you have a well-developed plan. Once you have a plan, meet quarterly to review the plan.

Disaster Recovery Assistance

If disaster does hit your library system, there is help. There are businesses around the country that specialize in disaster recovery for libraries. They handle major disasters from floodwaters, to fires, to mold. Call your state library association, search the Web, and ask for references from your insurance provider when disaster strikes. Ask for help. Do not try to solve a major disaster by yourself. Check references before you sign a contract with a disaster recovery service. Work closely with your superintendent, your supervisor, and the business office.

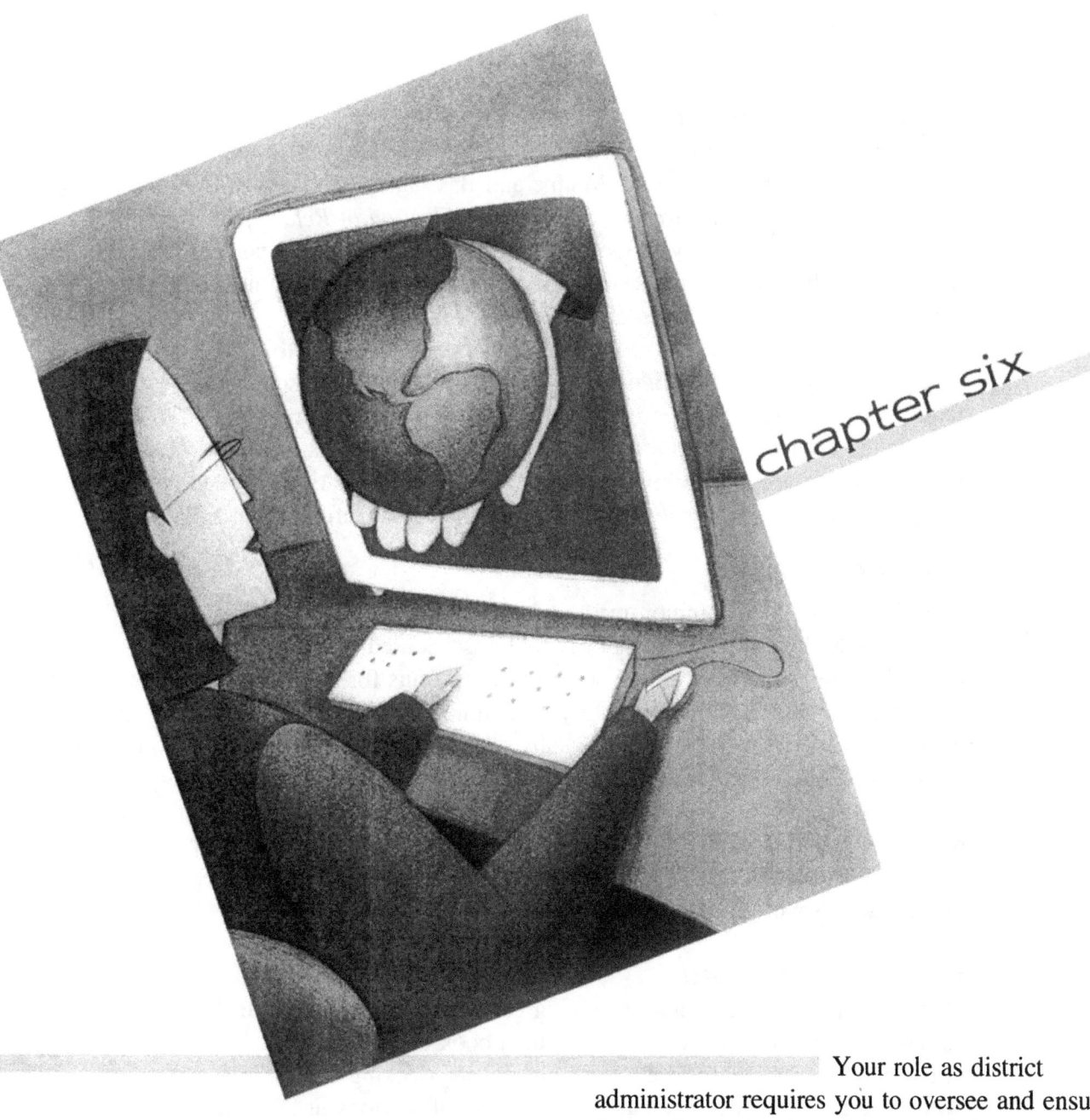

chapter six

Programming

Your role as district administrator requires you to oversee and ensure the quality and appropriateness of the programming presented in district libraries. Your vision and leadership will shape the future for the district's library media centers.

System-Wide Class Scheduling System

At the elementary level, the choice of scheduling format is usually between fixed schedules, flexible scheduling, and a combination of flexible and fixed. There are advantages and disadvantages to each. The library media director's job is to lobby for and oversee the scheduling of libraries.

Flexible Scheduling

In this type of scheduling system, classes are booked on an as-needed basis. According to survey results of J. Michie and B. Chaney in *Assessment of the Role of School and Public Libraries in Support of Education at Reform*, about 95 percent of public secondary school library media centers and 60 percent of public elementary school library media centers use flexible scheduling, most often in combination with regular fixed scheduling as well.

The librarian must have a good set of marketing skills to make flexible scheduling work. The librarian must be constantly out in the school connecting with teachers, selling the library program, and co-planning with teachers in order to keep the library program thriving. Principals with schools who have flexible library scheduling typically expect a high level of collaboration between the librarians and classroom teachers and understand the benefits of that collaboration.

Fixed Scheduling

Fixed scheduling is a common method for school librarian scheduling. Under this system, each class in an elementary school is scheduled into the library at a particular time, each week of the school year. A plus for this system is that each class in the school is assured a library class time each week, with the full attention of the librarian. The class time is usually divided between a library lesson and library checkout. The librarian is usually the person who designs the library lessons, hopefully with input from the classroom teachers. A potential drawback of fixed scheduling is that the more scheduled classes a library media specialist has, the less time she has to meet collaboratively with the classroom teachers and to work with small groups of students doing research projects.

Flexible and Fixed

Starting with a fixed schedule for seeing each class in the school for library lessons and checkout, the librarian can then book classes in for additional sessions in the library. This works well when classes are working on research projects and need extra library time. The larger the number of sections in the school, the less flexibility there is in booking additional classes into the library. Open checkout is usually available for students regardless of the type of scheduling.

There are pros and cons to both methods. The choice is up to you, your librarians, and the building administrators.

System-Wide Calendar

Using the school district calendar as soon as it is published for the following school year, begin to plan and book the library events, meetings, and celebrations. For instance, once you have the school calendar, fill in the district conference days, school improvement days, professional development days, early dismissals, winter and spring breaks. Once that is done, add the national library celebrations in which your libraries participate such as Children's Book Week, National Library Week, and Banned Books Week. That calendar can then be posted on your district library Web page and/or in the library media handbook/Web page for librarians, principals, and teachers to use.

Curriculum Design

The library media director must ensure that an extensive scope of appropriate services is offered in the school library. The library should offer students meaningful and well-planned lessons that prepare students to harvest and utilize information from the printed text—from the cover to the index. Students must learn how to locate, analyze, and use information. The underlining goal of the instruction provided in the library is to help students gain independent skills of study and investigation and promote lifelong investigation, learning, and literacy.

The library curriculum must be designed to target these meaningful goals and as to assist students in mastering the necessary skills to perform well in life, as well as on local, state, and national assessment tests. The library media director and school librarians must serve on curriculum design teams in order to work closely with teachers in curriculum development.

The development of the library curriculum for your school district is up to you and your team. As you develop the specific library curriculum you will want to do some research and a needs assessment. You will want to know what the librarians, teachers, and administrators in your district think belong in the library curriculum. You will want to consult the information literacy standards.

The library curriculum should be a written document organized by grade level. It should be written by a team of librarians at each level, be aligned with subject area curriculum, and with state and national standards. Once written, make it available on the district Web page and in hard copy.

The American Association of School Libraries (AASL) has identified critical thinking skills and information literacy standards in *Information Power* (AASL/AECT) at <<www.ala.org/acrl/ilcomstan.html>>. They are widely accepted in our schools.

Plagiarism

As your librarians work with teachers to assist students with research projects, one topic they may face is that of potential student plagiarism. School districts need a system to uncover plagiarism. Some schools and some districts invest in software that analyzes student research papers for plagiarism. Some of the services available for purchase are:

- EVE2 (Essay Verification Engine)
  <<http://www.canexus.com/eve/index.shtml>>
- Glatt Plagiarism Services
  <<http://www.lplagiarism.com/>>
- Turnitin:com
  <<http://www.turnitin.com>>
- MyDropBox.com
  <<http://mydropbox.com/>>
- EduTie.com
  <<http://www.edutie.com/>>

Database Searching

Students must learn how to search the online databases that you offer them. You and your staff should develop an easy-to-follow brochure or guide sheet to assist students in their use of the databases.

Assessment Methods for Library Skills

The librarians need methods to measure how students are learning the library curriculum. One typical method is the administration by the school district of nationally normed tests. Whether the Iowa Test of Basic Skills (ITBS) or Iowa Test of Education Development (ITED), the National Assessment of Educational Performance (NAEP), the Stanford Achievement Test (SAT 10), or any other nationally normed test is given, you will have formal feedback on student achievement in library related skills.

Informal assessment should be an ongoing process used by the school librarians. They observe students during each class period and can get feedback to determine which students have mastered particular skills and which students will require more instruction. Some librarians are required to assign grades to library work. Some are also required to assign grades for report cards.

More formal evaluation of skill mastery is achieved when students have produced a product such as a multimedia presentation, a formal report, or a research project. Many districts have established guidelines and grade levels where projects will be required. A district committee of subject area specialists, librarians, and administrators develops scoring rubrics. These rubrics are designed to measure the students' progress toward established objectives. Consider your district and state technology standards as well as the ISTE (International Society for Technology in Education) standards so that you can fold those expectations and skills into the requirements.

The establishment of these projects and the development of the scoring rubrics take time and district-wide effort to match to state and national standards and to encompass the broad range of subject area goals and objectives, along with the integration of technology and information literacy skills. Allow yourself plenty of time to collaborate with teachers, librarians, and administrators to develop such projects. It is critical that all of the stakeholders are included in the planning process.

Supporting the District Reading Program

The library media program in your school district should be congruent with and a vehicle for delivery of the school district's reading program. From purchasing the library materials recommended by the adopted reading text, to using same and similar graphic organizers and comprehension strategies, the library media specialists should be an integral part of the school's reading program. Your job is to see that this is the practice in your schools. Monitoring long-range library lesson plans and conducting formal and informal observations are two ways you can monitor this process.

Another way to monitor the reading program is to establish "Best Practices" study groups with the librarians. Choose some professional books that you think represent best practices in reading instruction. Offer the titles to the study group of librarians and let them choose the ones they wish to read. After they have read the books, have them share practical ideas that they got from the books and any materials that they developed to use in library lessons. Your leadership lights the way with the selection of professional books and motivating librarians to join you in the study groups. The librarians take a leadership role when they make the strategies their own and embed the practices in their library lessons.

See an example of what two librarians in Olathe, Kansas shared at a regional conference for librarians in Appendix G. The handout, entitled *Linking Literature to Text Structure Activities*, matches types of graphic organizers librarians can use to teach comprehension with the titles of some books that are very helpful in the use of the graphic organizers.

The reading instruction program works diligently to teach children the skills of reading. The library provides the materials and the inspiration for children to practice the skills they are learning and to begin to become lifelong readers. Teaching the skills of reading without constantly emphasizing the practice of reading is a little like saddling up but never riding the horse. Help librarians ignite and keep the fire of loving to read alive in the students. Continue to motivate librarians to use the strategies and activities that cause students to be motivated to read and to learn. For example, teach the techniques of sustained silent reading and use it regularly in the library, give inspirational book talks regularly, and hold reading promotion contests and games.

Lance, Welborn and Hamilton-Pennel in their 1993 study *The Impact of School Library Media Centers on Academic Achievement* showed that students in schools where the library media specialist took an instructional role by either finding the instructional materials and sharing them with teachers in planning units or by collaborating with teacher in planning instructional units, tended to score better in reading.

Encourage librarians to systematically make connections with subject area teachers in order to ensure student mastery of the curriculum objectives. Librarians have different systems for making sure this happens. Two librarians have developed a record system method. One page of this is shown in Appendix H entitled *Instruction to Support Curricular Objectives—English*.

The library is the place to broaden students' interests and horizons by offering a rich variety of appealing materials, both fiction and non-fiction, on many reading levels and topics. The librarian must post displays and bulletin boards, give book talks, and promote the best of children's and young adult literature in order to entice the reluctant reader. Frequent visits to the libraries, the inservice you offer, and positive feedback about the efforts librarians are making in this area will help staff keep the focus.

Another area where the director's leadership is needed is in collaborating with the local public library. Build bridges with the public library. Collaborate frequently. See if there are ways that you can pool or share resources, professional development opportunities, speakers, and visiting authors. Keep the public library informed of curriculum and homework needs and encourage librarians to schedule and coordinate class visits to the library. The cooperative relationship between the public library and the school system is beneficial to students, teachers, and the community.

Designing Technology Literacy Standards

Your district probably has a set of technology standards. If not, a reasonable place to start is with International Society for Technology Education (ISTE). Their Web page is <<http://cnets.iste.org/students/s_stands.html>>. Many other examples of technology standards can be found on the Internet. The standards typically require students to apply critical thinking skills in order to organize and use information they have received from a variety of sources, including electronic technology. Students need to be able to access, evaluate, and analyze information in a variety of forms and then use in it a purposeful manner. Do a search to find samples that might work for you and your school district.

Online Catalog

Students and staff must learn to use the online catalog. You can assist this effort by developing easy-to-use materials for librarians to use with students. Consider having one of the library committees, such as the multimedia committee, produce a multimedia presentation on using your online catalog. Once it is made, post it on your district library Web page so librarians have easy access to it.

Librarians will need comprehensive manuals for using the different staff modules in your library management system. Training materials are probably available from the software vendor from whom you purchased the system. The availability of easy-to-use, comprehensive manuals for staff use is certainly a consideration when choosing a library management system.

Collaborating With Teachers

One of the highest priorities the school librarians must have is that of collaborating with teachers. The benefits of that collaboration are seen both in the research and in the field. Librarians need to establish collegial, collaborative relationships with teachers. Where the librarian and the teacher work together, students benefit. Your role is to encourage collaboration by:

- Spotlighting places where it is done well
- Showing how busy librarians manage to make it a high priority
- Setting up discussion groups about it
- Featuring stories on it in your newsletters and TV programming
- Cross pollinating great examples of collaboration

Since the research shows that collaboration between the librarian and the teacher is critical to student achievement, in your role as supervisor, you will work with the library media specialists to develop strong bonds with the classroom teachers in their buildings.

Many elementary librarians use a monthly curriculum guide to assist classroom teachers in delivering instruction with the proper materials. Figure 6.1, Library Monthly Curriculum, is an example of one.

Figure 6.1

Teacher _____

Library Monthly Curriculum Integration for September

Language Arts	Social Studies	Science/ Health	Math	Special Projects (Reports, research, etc.)	Would you like to meet with me?
Topic	Topic	Topic	Topic	Topic	Date: Time:
Materials needed?	Materials needed?	Materials needed?	Materials needed?	Materials needed?	Materials needed?
Circle:	Circle:	Circle:	Circle:	Circle:	Circle:
Books	Books	Books	Books	Books	Books
Videos	Videos	Videos	Videos	Videos	Videos
Read-Alongs	Read-Alongs	Read-Alongs	Read-Alongs	Read-Alongs	Read-Alongs
Teaching/ Instructional Activities	Teaching/ Instructional Activities	Teaching/ Instructional Activities	Teaching/ Instructional Activities	Teaching/ Instructional Activities	Teaching/ Instructional Activities
Web Sites	Web Sites	Web Sites	Web Sites	Web Sites	Web Sites

At the secondary school level, librarians must be constantly marketing their offerings to classroom teachers in order to establish collaboration. See *Instruction to Support Curricular Objectives – English* in Appendix H for a sample of one way for librarians to connect with teachers and for you to monitor that effort.

Special Events

Many school districts fund and plan special events for school libraries such as author visits and writer's workshops. Your leadership is needed in the development of special events. You may need to write a grant or two, establish some business or community partnerships, or otherwise find funding and assistance to establish and foster these programs. Two examples of library special events are author/illustrator visits and writer's workshops.

Special Programming

The needs of your community may guide you in establishing special programming to fit the unique needs. Some examples are noted.

- *No Child Left Behind* — A huge component of *NCLB* is parent involvement. Library programming and literacy initiatives are a natural fit for involving parents in the school. From designing your libraries to include spaces for young children and their parents to engage in age-appropriate activities; to scheduling events to promote literacy for parents and children; to purchasing materials such as games, art supplies, and toys, you need a district plan to involve families in your school libraries. Expand the role of the school library to nurture life-long learning and literacy by building bridges between the home and the school.
Community reading promotions are another way to promote literacy and family involvement in your schools. There are many models for these promotions that you may use as you plan yours.
- *Title I Schools* — Involving parents in the school is an ongoing effort in Title I schools. Developing library programming that draws parents into the school can be a cornerstone in the school plan to involve parents. It is an opportunity to level the playing field and give low-income children and families a literacy boost.
- *English Language Learners (ELL)* — Another effort you may wish to make on a district level is programming to assist with family literacy in school communities where English is not the first language. Refugee and immigrant families can teach the schools customs, dance steps, recipes for native dishes, while they learn their ABC's and how to speak English.
By partnering with a local entity such as a community college, the school librarian can offer literacy programming for the children while a college instructor teaches English to parents and family members. Effective programs usually offer parent education, student education, parent/child together time, and a parenting skills component. Planning from the district level can make this type of

program a reality for your community.
- *Multilevel Programming*—Another district-wide initiative to consider is that of offering multilevel programming. High school students working with middle school students or elementary students in literacy projects can be beneficial to students at both levels. Cadets from high school can work with emergent readers at the primary level. High school students who are immigrants and have mastered English can work with new immigrants to the country. Projects like this need vision and coordination from the district level.
- *Extended Hours*—Some school districts offer extended hours before and after school, on the weekends, and in the summer. The issues involved in offering extended hours are:

  - Staffing
  - Costs
  - Security
  - Funding Sources

The benefits to offering extended hours have been studied. Those studies show that increased time spent in the school library media center increases student achievement and literacy. One such study is: Keith Curry Lance, et al., *Measuring Up to Standards: The Role of School Libraries and Information Literacy.*

Researchers looking at out-of school programs, both after school and in the summer, result in academic gains for low-achieving and at-risk students. "The Effectiveness of Out-Of-School-Time Strategies in Assisting Low-Achieving Students in Reading and Mathematics: A Research Synthesis" is online at www.mcrel.org.

Program costs vary according to the number of staff members needed to staff the library and the number of extended hours offered. Providing student access to computers for those who do not have them at home can make a big difference to the potential digital divide. The digital divide is a term used frequently to describe the gap in opportunities between families who own and use current computer technology and those who do not.

According to Stephen Krashen's study, *The Power of Reading: Insights from the Research*, "greater access to the school library media center was correlated with a higher rate of voluntary reading and academic achievement. Larger collections and longer hours increase both circulation and reading, which in turn increases reading comprehension, vocabulary growth, grammatical usage, spelling ability, and writing style."

Summer Library
Consider writing a federal 21st Century Community Learning Center Grant to fund your program. Find information at <<http://www.ed.gov/programs/21stcclc/index.html>>.

One solution to funding a summer library program can be finding sponsorship. Corporations in your area might be interested in funding the summer library program and so might your individual Parent Teacher Associations. Writing a grant or working with your local public library can also be funding sources. Refer to Anderson's *Write Grants, Get Money* (2002) for assistance.

Program Evaluation

The ALA book *Information Power: Building Partnerships for Learning* will be an excellent resource for you as you make your plans for program evaluation. It is important to be able to show the impact that your library programs have on your students and staff. Another good resource is a book called *Program Evaluation: Library Media Services* by the National Study of School Evaluation (NSSE). Work with your team to determine how you will evaluate the effectiveness of your programs. Then, share that information in order to promote the positive impact you are having.

Encourage librarians to produce end of year reports for their school libraries. This one or two page document should show:

- The circulation statistics this year compared to last year
- The holdings report
- The budget report with a breakout of collection development goals for the year
- Collection analysis with strengths and growth areas
- Student achievement scores in reading this year compared to last
- Special programming during the year
- Any additional funding such as grants and donations
- Goals for the coming year

Ask librarians to use this report to keep the principal, the parents, the friends of the library, the PTA, the staff, and the students informed about the library and its accomplishments for the year. Show the vitality of the libraries and market their programming and achievements.

State and National Standards

Check with your state department of education to learn if your state has state standards for libraries. If they do, you must take those into consideration as you plan your library curriculum, programs, and facilities. For information about national standards, see *Information Power: Building Partnerships for Learning*.

District Resource Centers

District centers can maintain resource materials in all curricular areas for teacher checkout. They can house resources and staff who support the librarians and teachers in areas such as purchasing, processing materials, and managing a booking system for district-level media checkout. Appendix I, *Indian Creek Brochure*, shows one example of services offered at a district resource center.

chapter seven

Technology

Recent research by Keith Curry Lance, Marcia Rodney, and Christine Hamilton-Pennell, shows that students in schools with technologically advanced libraries performed up to 18 percent higher on statewide tests than peers in schools with poorly equipped libraries. This data is a compelling reason to examine your current technology status and set some goals for the future.

Long-Range Library Technology Plan

A technology plan is an integral part of your library long-range plan. Without a long-range plan for technology, you do not qualify to apply for E-rate funding. Although it may be difficult to predict technology needs very far into the future, because technology changes so rapidly, some type of prediction must be done.

Selecting and Purchasing Library Technology

There are many factors to consider when selecting and purchasing library technology, such as:

- Know where you are before you start to buy more
- Do not forget to factor power sources and needs into the equation
- Allow your software needs to dictate your hardware needs
- Ask software vendors for advice
- Make sure the IT department purchases what teachers need, not what IT thinks they need
- Keep it uniform; do not allow renegade equipment
- Decide what type of extended warranties you want and do not be swayed by the vendor's sales pitch
- Buy the most powerful hardware you can afford
- Consider future growth, increases in enrollment, and storing more information
- Establish a purchasing and replacement schedule
- Make sure there is flexibility in your schedule
- Pay careful attention to network security
- Do not forget assistive technology for patrons with special needs
- Beware of accepting used, donated hardware as it may not be powerful enough or compatible with district hardware

Tracking Fixed Assets

You will need a method of tracking fixed assets in the various libraries. Your state law and district policies will probably dictate the types of equipment that you need to track and the times you need to inventory. The typical time frame for inventorying fixed assets is once a year. The types of equipment and furniture you are required to track can vary. Usually equipment, such as computers purchased with capital funds at a cost above a certain amount, have to be tracked. The most common method of tracking them is by attaching a unique barcode when they are assigned a location within your district and then using a scanner to read the barcodes once a year. Keep careful records of the inventory findings and file the proper paperwork.

Library Management Software

There are many companies that supply library automation systems. Go to the Web and search for library automation software to find them.

See *Chapter Three* for selection criteria and tips on purchasing library management software. Automation vendors have visions for how automation software can continue to improve for the future. Currently, many vendors are trying to provide easy and comprehensive access from a variety of sources, such as laptops and hand-held devices.

Other Software

You may be responsible at the district level for selecting and possibly maintaining the computer software collection for the school libraries. You will want to carefully evaluate software before you purchase it and you will want input from many voices before you choose.

Vendors are good about offering free trials for librarians to get acquainted with their products. One selection method is to have all librarians preview the products and choose the top three to bring to the library advisory committee. Another way is to have the library advisory committee evaluate and then offer their top choices to all librarians to make a recommendation for purchase.

If you are selecting databases for elementary, middle, and high school levels, you will want to consider purchasing all three levels from the same vendor. The vendors offer discounts when you bundle levels and schools. Another advantage is that similar formats make it easier to teach and learn them. Consider teaming with another school district or local public library to consolidate purchasing power and to have more leverage with the vendors. Investigate forming a consortium with them to establish greater buying power in the market.

You will want to develop a scoring rubric to use as you evaluate software for district-wide purchase. Use your library advisory committee and/or your library technology committee for a meaningful way to arrive at a comprehensive rubric. There are many factors to consider such as price, quality, accuracy, meeting curriculum needs, and completeness.

Internet Access

Working with your information services department, you will want to provide the fastest, most reliable, most secure Internet access that you can for your patrons. The size of your district, number of schools, geographic location, access to technology, and budget will all influence the type of Internet access you choose.

E-Rate

The Universal Service Administrative Company's Schools and Libraries Division administers the E-rate program. They offer funding for schools and libraries for Internet and telecommunications services. The application process is difficult, but well worth the effort for the funding. The federal government gives about $2.25 billion each year to schools and public libraries through discounts on technology and Internet access.

Filing for E-rate discounts can be an arduous task. Because of the complexity of the application process, some people recommend not combining your applications for separate services. They recommend applying for each type of service separately so that if something is wrong with one of your applications, you might lose only that funding, not all of it. They do have a help desk with well-trained staff who can answer your questions. There is an appeal process in case your application is not funded, but be prepared to be patient with the process.

You will need a district technology plan in place before you can apply and you will need to have an Internet filtering system in place before receiving any funds. For more information on the E-rate check the eligible services list at http://sL.universalservice.org/reference/eligible.asp.

Internet Filtering and CIPA

The Children's Internet Protection Act (CIPA) requires schools and libraries to install a technology protection measure to protect children from undesirable and obscene online content. Schools who fail to comply with this act will lose federal subsidies from the E-rate. While there are concerns about the effectiveness of Internet filters, about 74 percent of K-12 schools use the filters.

District Library Web Page

While the information technology department of your school district has many responsibilities, overseeing the design and maintenance of the district library Web site should be on the shoulders of the library media director. On this site you should consider offering:

- Access to your online card catalog
- Portals to your licensed online databases
- Links to educational Web sites you deem appropriate
- Approved bibliographic formats for students to use
- Links to virtual reference desks

Library Web Pages

District librarians are sometimes asked to design and post library Web pages for each school library. A terrific resource for the school librarians to use as they produce and update their school library Web pages is the Linworth publication *Tooting Your Own Horn: Web-Based Public Relations for the 21st Century Librarian* by Julieta Dias Fisher and Ann Hill. Also take a look at *K-12 Web Pages: Planning and Publishing Excellent School Web Sites* by Debra Kay Logan and Cynthia Lee Beuselinck.

Some of the things librarians may wish to include on their school library Web pages are:

- Virtual tour of the library
- Tutorials and guides
- Library newsletter (current and past editions)
- Special collections and online exhibits
- Special forms
- Photos of events and people in the library
- Links to databases and online resources
- Links to age and curriculum appropriate Web sites
- Links to the local public library
- Links to faculty members and contact information

There are many outstanding school library Web pages on the Internet to use as models as you design your own. Lawrence High School Library is just one example of an effective school library Web page. See it at <<http://library.lhs.usd497.org/home.html>>.

Wide and Local Area Networks

School districts typically assign the responsibility of keeping the school district networks running to the information technology department. Preventing virus attacks and breaches of security, and preserving network bandwidth are additional responsibilities that fall to the information services department. Although you may not be responsible for information technology services, you must work closely and cooperatively with the staff that perform the information technology services for the district. Become a problem solver and a diplomatic negotiator for your students and staff.

If your school district has a wide area network (WAN), you will probably want the library collection databases on that network in order for each library to have access to the district union catalog. If you do not have a wide area network and you want one, work with your information services technology department and with your superintendent to describe the benefits of a wide area network.

Many districts prefer to network library computers in each building on a local area network (LAN). If that is your preference, work with your information services technology manager to explore the possibilities for your libraries.

Wireless labs and laptops seem to go together. When a class of students is using laptops in the library and each one is connected to a wall with cables, there is the safety factor of tripping over them and the hazard of the laptop cords being ripped from the walls while the computers are still connected to the wall.

Technology Standards

If your state and or school district has technology standards for students and or staff, make sure that your library curriculum includes the requisite and appropriate technology skills and that you have the hardware and software necessary for students to use to reach the standards. Those standards impact the technology hardware and software requirements in your libraries. Become familiar with the technology standards that govern your state and your district, and make the librarians familiar with them.

Library Security Systems

High school libraries and many middle school libraries invest in some type of security system to manage theft of materials from the libraries. There are two types of systems. One type uses electromagnetically charged strips or disks inserted into the library materials that trigger an alarm in a security station when the materials are not properly checked out. One vendor of this type of systems is 3M™ In conjunction with AASL, they offer an annual grant for school libraries. Information about this grant can be found at the American Association of School Librarians Web page at <<www.ala.org>> or at <<www.3M.com/library>>.

Another type of system is a new technology called radio-frequency identification (RFID). This system claims to work faster and have more uses than the electromagnetically charged system. This type of system is about three times more expensive that the other and can be found more often in academic and public libraries.

Video Streaming and Digital Video

This type of technology has much to offer school library patrons. It offers more flexibility for viewing, and the indexing alone can speed up research. Still frames enhance multimedia presentations, but read the user licenses carefully to ensure copyright compliance. Unless otherwise specified, digital video may be used for instructional purposes such as research, criticism, and demonstration.

Instructional Media

A question many are asking is should we continue purchasing videos and VCRs or should we be investing in DVD players and DVDs? No one has a crystal ball to foretell the future, but there are facts we can examine. Around 250,000 VCRs continue to be produced and purchased each year. You cannot record from television to DVD, and there is still no cost effective recording device to record from a VCR to a DVD. A DVD is a fragile type of software that can be easily scratched.

DVDs are easy to use because of chaptering and they are easier to store since they take less space than videos. The picture quality is better on a DVD. Many people are compromising by purchasing dual-purpose hardware—VCR/DVD players and are beginning to add DVDs to their collections.

Instructional Television Programming

Many school districts opt to purchase annual subscriptions to broadcast or duplicate instructional programming tapes for distribution to schools. If your local public television station offers these subscriptions, look into the types of programming they offer, the quality of the programming, the match to your curriculum, and the cost. If you plan to invest in this subscription opportunity, you will want input and buy-in from the librarians, the curriculum department, the superintendent, and all involved in the commitment.

Instructional Television Production

Many school districts have a central instructional television production center. Some have TV production studios in the high schools. There are many facets to an ITV production center and the set-ups vary widely.

You may find yourself in a position to set up a production room. The simple version would have a room wired with closed-circuit TV, cable TV connections, satellite connections, VHS camera(s), lighting, microphones, sets such as a news desk, interview chairs, etc, or backdrops.

Elementary schools enjoy producing news broadcasts each morning to start the school day. From announcing the day's menu in the cafeteria, to the daily weather report, to promos for good books, the students can handle both the lights, camera, direction and announcing with just a little help from adults.

Secondary schools can produce that type of daily broadcast as well as special features such as news shows about the school's programs and people. If the district offers radio and TV classes at the secondary level, there are probably facilities for these classes already in existence.

Video is increasingly used both by students in their projects and by teachers as a method of instructional delivery. If that is the case in your school district, you should provide video editing equipment. Format decisions must be made before purchasing the editing equipment. Will you need analog (VHS, 8mm, Hi8) capacity or digital video (DV) or both? Along with the hardware, make sure you have editing software that is compatible with your video editor.

Digital Divide

Until all students have access to computers and the Internet, both at home and at school, there will continue to be an unequal opportunity for our students to learn. This unequal opportunity is often labeled a gap or the digital divide. Andrew Gordon, professor at the University of Washington and director of the Public Access Computing Project states, "As we become increasingly reliant on computers, the importance of the divide will increase." Public Access Computing Project. Andrew Gordon. University of Washington. <<http://www.gspa.Washington.edu/research/current.html#access>>. The acquisition of computers and Internet access needs to be wrapped with training and support in the use of them, if we want to close the digital gap. The school library can be the ideal spot to begin to close the digital gap and your leadership can make that happen.

Professional Growth and Development

Long-Range Professional Development Plan

In *Chapter 2* the need for a long-range or five-year plan for your library system was discussed and recommended. Part of that strategic plan should outline the plan for staff development in your library system. If you have not yet developed a long-range strategic plan, an excellent place to start is with professional growth, with the help of the district's staff development department.

What are the goals for your libraries? What are the district-wide goals? Once those goals are written, establish the timeframe for accomplishing those goals. What kind of training will staff members need to achieve those goals? What specifically is it that they need to know or be able to do? These complicated questions deserve thoughtful study on your part and input from the people you supervise and represent. Use the district's long-range plan as a blueprint for library staff development.

Professional Development Committee

A professional development committee is a vehicle for developing a training plan. Choose committee members from the librarians and library support staff, where applicable, at each level of school. Your school district probably has set aside days or partial days in the school calendar for staff professional development. It is your responsibility to plan programs for those days for the library staff. Doing that with the help of the professional development committee can make sure that the offerings meet the needs of the participants, the librarians buy-in to them, and the sessions hit the target.

When planning your committee meetings, be sure to have an agenda and ask ahead of time for input from the attendees. Set starting and ending times and honor them.

Make sure the room is set up in a way that is comfortable for all. For a truly open discussion, arrange chairs in a circle with a small break for flip charts. Offer something to drink or eat, when appropriate. Start with introductions and celebrations of recent accomplishments of the programs and people assembled. Take notes for the minutes right on your agenda so that you can send the minutes out later to all the librarians. Gracefully keep the group on task. Keep the pace frisky and use visuals when you can.

Following the meeting, be sure to send out the minutes of the meeting in a timely manner and follow through with any promises you made during the meeting. If you have electronic mail, send them that way for greater efficiency. Keep and file hard copies of the agendas and minutes for future reference.

Conducting Staff Development Needs Assessment

If your school district has a staff development department, you will want to work in tandem with those staff members to develop your needs assessment. Your state department of education or your state school library association may already have developed a school library staff development needs assessments. If so, take a look at those and see if administering one of them will serve you and your district. Another resource is an Internet search.

It is vital that your staff development plans are based on the specific needs of the students and staff as reflected in the needs assessment you conduct. Identify the needs and prioritize them so that participants see these opportunities as relevant and valuable. That in turn will create buy-in from staff and motivate them to attend the sessions and to implement the learning. Begin looking at target results and then do task analysis to help you move toward reaching those target goals.

Results-Based Staff Development

It is important to make sure that the staff development offerings that you plan are results-based. According to the National Staff Development Council, results-based staff development is "staff development that results in improved performance by students, staff and the organization. The success of staff development should be measured by whether it alters instructional behavior in a away that benefits students."

In an effort to determine what professional development classes to offer you must determine the following:

- What are the student goals?
- Where is current student performance?
- What are the identified student learning indicators that must be taught?
- What are the staff skills that are needed to help students learn the indicated skills and information?
- What are the staff's current skills?
- What are the professional development needs?
- What are the district's goals?

The levels of teachers' skills in results-based terms are:

Teacher/Librarian has awareness of the skill or concept – She is developing and awareness and building knowledge. She knows something she did not know before.

Teacher/Librarian demonstrates the skill in practice—She consistently now uses this knowledge or skill in her job.

Teacher/Librarian integrates the skill into lessons—This newly acquired skill is having an impact on student learning. Learning is improving as measured on assessment aligned with specific improvement goals.

Teacher/Librarian transfers the learning into a new setting—She can take the skill and apply it in a different situation and have a direct positive impact on student learning.

When planning results-based staff development, you will want to outline several things. The first is teacher/librarian results. What do librarians need to know and be able to do? For example, librarians need to use a variety of research-based strategies to increase students' use of before, during and after-reading strategies. Second, what evidence will show that the strategies are being applied? Examples might be data from the librarian's long-range plans, daily lesson plans, and formal observations. Third, what will the student indicators be? How will the implementation of this plan effect student learning? An example would be that student test scores in reading comprehension on state assessments improve.

To create a results-based staff development program you should consider the following:

- Staff development goals
- Staff development strategies
- Timeline
- Person(s) responsible
- Resources needed
- Indicators/evaluation

See Appendix J for an example of a results-based staff development plan. If you would like to learn more about this topic, there are many books to read on results-based staff development.

Planning Staff Development

As you plan effective staff development, keep in mind that people learn in different and similar ways. Some of what we know about learning theory tells us that:

- Active learners are more engaged and learn better.
- Active participation increases learning.
- New learning requires massed practice followed by distributed practice.
- Feedback or knowledge of results is critical to learning.
- New learning is fragile.

As you plan sessions, remember to divide the material into learning segments. Write performance objectives for each segment. What will the learner be able to do at the conclusion of the session as a result of the class offering? Use the phrase "the learner will" to start your objectives followed by what the learner will be able to do as a result of the lesson. Example: The learner will develop a library reading lesson teaching fact and opinion for fifth grade students.

Plan to actively involve the learners in course objectives. Set the ground rules and get buy-in:

- Listen actively
- Everyone participates
- Seek to understand
- Honor time limits
- Express support when you agree
- Have fun and be creative

Encourage your participants to take notes and to honor one another as they learn. Give participants ample opportunities for hands-on engagement in professional development and allot the necessary time for practice before expecting learners to employ the new strategies and learning. Be sure that the practice is embedded in the sessions.

Plan Ahead and Be Organized

When planning staff development programs, plan, plan, and then plan some more. Make checklists for all of the arrangements and make sure that your cast of players knows their roles. Prepare your handouts and multimedia presentations and proofread them multiple times. If you are holding the training session off-site, be sure to have all of your training materials packed in a convenient, portable, and easy to access manner.

Types of Staff Development

There are many ways to deliver staff development. As leader, consider all of the possibilities and decide which you feel are the most effective for your staff. The times that you will have the undivided attention of the librarians and library staff will probably be few and consequentially precious to you. You will want to get the most bang for the buck that you can from your staff development offerings.

Lectures—Consultants, experts, professors, and others are available to share research and experience in a lecture format. This format works well in a large setting such as a national convention but might not be the best choice for your staff of three or four school librarians.

Field Trips—These can be very valuable. If your district is considering block scheduling at the high school level, you may wish to plan a field trip for your high school librarians to a school district nearby where block scheduling has been successfully implemented. Scout these field trips ahead of time so that you know the site is a good match to your vision and that the host librarian(s) know the objectives of the field trip.

Small Group Sharing—Professionals sharing in small interest-alike groups can be powerful learning experiences.

University Classes—There are online classes and brick and mortar classes. These tend to work well for individuals who are committed to improving their knowledge and skills in a learning setting outside the school library.

Online Tutorials—Many universities and organizations, such as the American Library Association (ALA), are offering online tutorials on a variety of topics.

Book Study Groups—Librarians choosing a book on pedagogy or another literacy/library topic read a particular book and meet to discuss it and exchange ideas.

Many types of activities can be included in your staff development sessions. A few ways to structure sessions are:

- Use role-playing or case studies
- Invite guest speakers or use a panel
- Brainstorm as a group
- Do visualization exercises
- Break into small groups for problem solving and concept development
- Offer self-scoring mini quizzes

As you plan inservice activities, be sure to assume that your participants have keen intelligence and have had rich experiences. Create a sense of well-being in the training sessions where trust can develop and participants can help one another. Be patient and understanding; everyone has a difficult job and difficult days. Walk the walk; don't just talk the talk. Model what you teach. Do not bore your participants and do not lecture. Make the learning pertinent and meaningful. Keep it short. Plan one or two key ideas per session and plan action steps to be taken immediately after each idea.

Professional Development Committee

Form a staff development committee to help you plan and deliver these opportunities. You will want librarians from all levels on your committee. As you look at the calendar for the school year, you will see the dates and times that your library team will have the opportunity to engage in professional development. Once you have determined which days and times are available for in-service, then you may begin to plan. If you have already conducted a needs assessment on staff development, provide that information to your planning team. If you have not conducted a needs assessment, this is another good time to do so.

Now is the time to tie your professional development to *No Child Left Behind* and to your students achieving Adequate Yearly Progress (AYP). Examine what the librarians can do to improve reading comprehension, vocabulary skills, and fluency. Keep those state and local benchmarks in mind as you plan. Focus on ideas that will improve student skills and competencies and therefore student achievement. Remember too that staff development offerings may be tied to licensure and professional development points in your school district.

Other Library Media Committees

Each full-time librarian should be on a committee in order to be a full participant in the district library media program. Committees are an opportunity for each librarian to receive staff development and to contribute to the leadership of your library program. Committees can meet quarterly, once each semester, or more often if you prefer. Meeting on contract time is ideal if you wish to have each librarian involved. In addition to interest-alike groups, you can also group by teaching level such as elementary, middle and high school groups. The meetings can be held in a central office location or at various school libraries. The choice is yours. A one-hour meeting duration is ideal.

The library advisory committee and the professional development committee have already been mentioned. In addition, consider the following other committees.

Library Technology Committee—Preview software, consult on Internet issues, acquire and teach multimedia production skills.
Library Gift Committee—Determine if gift materials are appropriate to be included in the school library. Materials must meet the same criteria as materials selected for purchase through regular district procedures.
Public Relations Committee—Plan activities for Children's Book Week, National Library Week, and for library social events.
Other District-Wide Committees

Opportunities

There are many opportunities to connect with other organizations and school districts to offer staff development for the librarians.

- Teleconferences
- Distance learning
- Out of district travel
    - Regional conferences
    - National conferences
- Local public libraries
- Neighboring school districts
- Online tutorials

Evaluation of Staff Development Sessions

Do not forget the evaluation component. Check to see if your district staff development department has a standard form for participants to fill out to evaluate a staff development session. If so, is it one that you can use for librarians to fill out following your session? If not, you will need to develop one. Developing one would be a good activity for your professional development committee. Search online for some examples.

Determine what areas you want to evaluate and how you plan to do that. Again, study examples to come up with a plan. As you design the grand plan for staff development, try to move to internally driven and designed sessions that are program-based and embraced by your staff. Plan for results and allow participants to reflect on their learning.

If you are following the principles of results-based staff development, you will know to build in a strong evaluation component to your offering. The evaluation component will be based on the learning outcomes and the achievement you want to see as a result of the sessions. Evaluating the results of your staff development efforts can pay off. You will learn what effect and impact the sessions are having on student achievement. Report the results you are getting to the policy makers in your district. Use the results to plan for the future.

You will want to examine both formative and summative evaluations as both will be valuable feedback to you.

Formative Evaluation—These evaluations are conducted during the life of a staff development program. It can improve the program, prevent problems in implementation, and help make sure that the program is functioning effectively.

Summative Evaluation—This type of evaluation is conducted at the end of a program. If the program is to last three to five years, you might want to do summative evaluation on it at the end of two or three years, or at the end of a funding cycle.

School Improvement Initiatives

You will want the school librarians with whom you work to be intimately involved with the school improvement initiatives in their schools. Assume that the school library is the heart of the school. The school librarian should be an integral part of the school improvement teams in each of the buildings. While you can't require librarians to volunteer to serve in that capacity, you can certainly inspire them to volunteer. As school librarians, these leaders should be purchasing the professional journals, books, and multimedia materials that support the learning quest that the improvement team is taking. The librarian should be the master at searching databases for the research on learning and teaching strategies to support the improvement plan. You can support that effort by offering staff development in that area.

One opportunity that is offered through AASL is the series of leadership institutes called "Leading Through Collaboration." It is possible for a school district to host an institute. For more information, log on to <<www.ala.org/aasl>>.

The Director's Professional Development and Growth

It is critical that you, as the director or supervisor of your system of school libraries, continue to pursue professional growth and development opportunities. While you may be the wind beneath the wings of the library staff, you also need to be a guiding light. You need to know what is current and what is coming in order to lead your system of libraries.

There are many opportunities out there that might interest you. If you have a long-range plan for your libraries, it should follow that you know what your long-range staff development goals are. Once you know those goals, it is easier to select the staff development opportunities that are most appropriate for you and your plan. Participate in your local, state and national library organizations and conferences. Not only should you be attending the meetings and conferences produced by these groups, you should be participating in the planning, organizing, and presenting.

Presenting at a conference is often as much of a learning experience as is attending a conference. Challenge yourself to apply to present at a local, regional, and/or national conference. If you are selected to present, you will find yourself researching, learning, and organizing your thoughts. Assembling the data and creating a multimedia presentation with handouts is a process that will stretch you professionally.

Credentials

Your credentials, and those of the librarians in your system, need to be up-to-date. Today's climate of mandating that all teachers are highly qualified has placed special interest in licensure, certification, and credentials. Many states are in the process of refining or changing their certification and licensure programs. Another responsibility of the central library media director is to ensure that the library staff has the proper credentials.

Learn what the requirements are in your state for your position and for the librarians and library aides, clerks, or paraprofessionals, where applicable. Examine your own credentials and those of the librarians.

Leadership

Focus in on leadership development. Develop the ability to take a broad, systemic view, to work effectively in a large system, to think creatively, and to learn from experience. Become self-aware and develop self-confidence as you plan to take a leadership role.

When working with others, maintain and enhance their self-esteem, listen and respond with empathy, ask for help, and encourage the involvement of others in leadership roles. To lead is to serve.

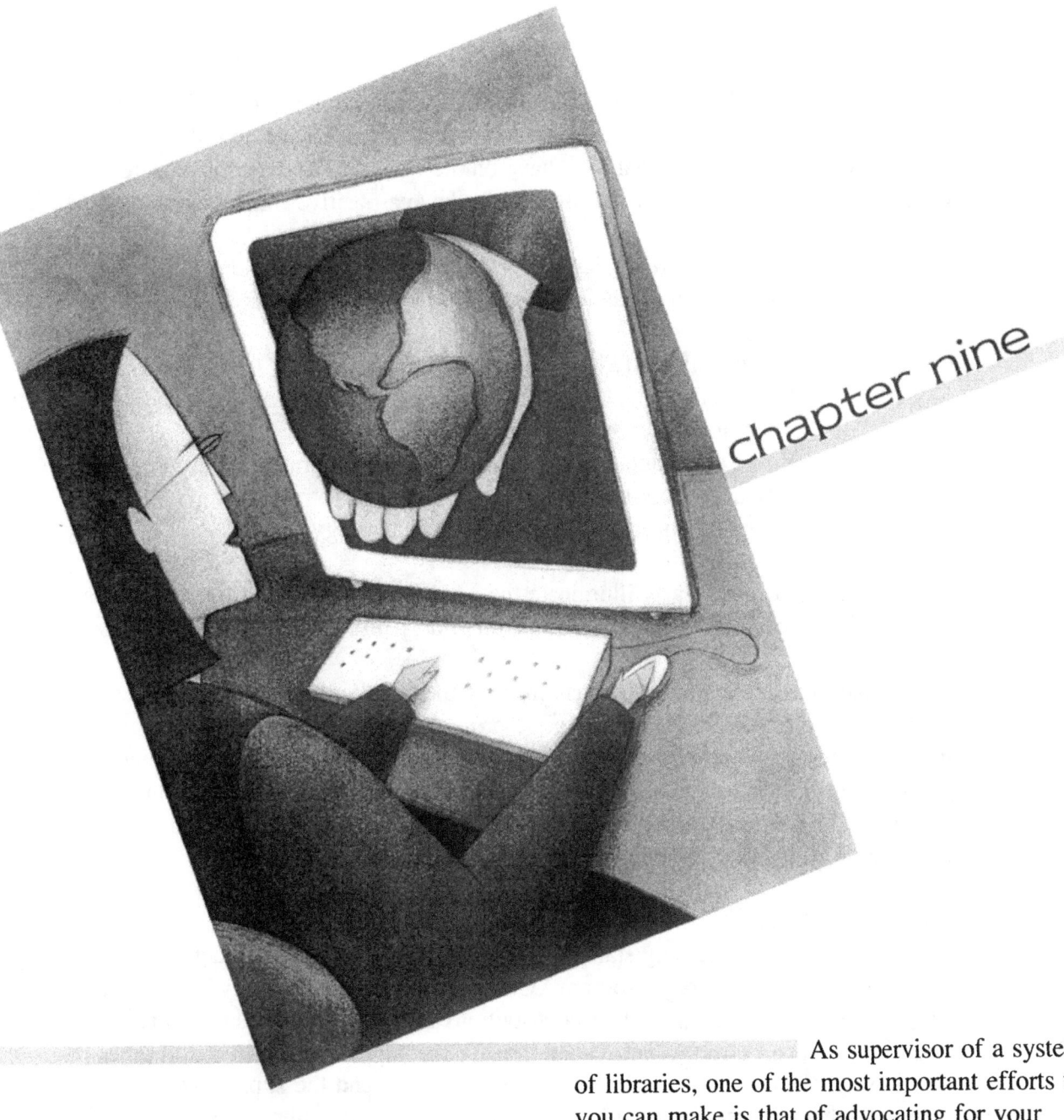

Advocacy

chapter nine

As supervisor of a system of libraries, one of the most important efforts that you can make is that of advocating for your libraries. You cannot assume for one minute that your library system will thrive, grow, or flourish without effective advocacy on the part of the leader. You must have ongoing, positive communications between your library system and your community. Dust off your public relations skills and step up onto the library advocacy platform.

Advocating for People

Librarians

Skilled, trained librarians are at the heart of effective libraries. Without certified, licensed professional librarians, our libraries cannot thrive.

The public doesn't always know that. One way we know that the public has a false perception is by what we read. Organizations often talk of how they no longer need librarians, now that they have online research databases and search engines. Research shows that school libraries have a positive impact on student performance.

In *How School Libraries Improve Outcomes for Children*, Lance, Rodney, and Hamilton-Pennell report that strong school library programs are:

- Adequately staffed, stocked, and funded
- Have staff who are actively involved leaders in their school's teaching and learning enterprise
- Have staff who are collegial, and have collaborative relationships with classroom teachers
- Embracing networked information technology

These findings clearly illuminate the need for strong school libraries. It is the job of the director to get this information widely disseminated into the community.

We must recognize librarians, promote them, celebrate them, and honor them whenever possible. The more good press the librarians and the programs get, the better your library system looks and the stronger it will be. Just being recognized for their hard work is often an incentive for employees to continue the hard work. Librarians are key to the literacy push in your school district. Advocate for them; let the public know their value.

Support Staff

The library clerks, processing staff, educational aides, and reading teachers are a valuable part of your library program. Once again, you are their advocate. You are in a position to recognize their contributions and to spotlight them whenever you can. Make an effort to get recognition for the support staff in your libraries. Attend the volunteer teas to salute both the volunteers and the support staff. Nominate them for service awards and feature them in your library newsletters.

Volunteers

Attracting and keeping library volunteers can be critical to the library programs. Whether they are members of the friends of the library or actual hands-on, daily volunteers, these people need the support of the library staff with whom they work, and they need reliable communication with the school system. Each of these volunteers goes out into the community to spread the good word about libraries, if they are treated well. They can be tremendous positive promoters of your program.

Promote volunteer recognition ceremonies with your librarians. Encourage the librarians to honor their volunteers often and well. Whether they offer a token gift of a votive candle at holiday time with a note attached, "You light the way for our readers!" or a volunteer tea in the library after school, complete with "golden" crowns for the royal volunteers, librarians need to thank their supporters. They need your encouragement to establish and maintain this practice.

Suggest a story about an outstanding volunteer to the local newspaper reporter. Do you have a volunteer in your system who brings a Civil War era letter and memorabilia collection for display in the library display case? This is the type of thing that a reporter can write about that will show appreciation for a volunteer while providing positive press for your library.

Community Leaders
The school board members, board of regents, legislators, key administrators and other community members should be targets of your positive advocacy of the library system. As the saying goes, "Perception is reality," and how the community leaders perceive you, your programs, and your staff is supremely important. If they see the librarians and the library programs as effective, dynamic, and a critical part of the education of children, you are in a good space and have a bright future. Do what you can to promote that positive perception. Work with your library advisory committee to determine methods and venues to spotlight your school libraries in the community.

Getting Positive Attention
There are many ways to promote your libraries. Seeking positive public recognition is one very important way. You need to give sustained effort to getting positive attention and recognition for your libraries. Publicize the educationally sound programming that is occurring in your libraries. Another way to focus on the positive things the libraries are doing is to ask librarians to submit a monthly report to you so that you can accumulate data about the libraries and report the positive news. See Appendix K and L for sample elementary and secondary monthly reports.

Enter Contests
Enter your libraries in contests. Does one of your libraries need a security system? How about applying to 3M™ to win a fantastic new library security system? If you win, you will get the new system plus some very positive public relations for your library. Entering contests does not usually require a great deal of effort, and the resulting positive attention for the librarians can be tremendous.

Apply for Awards
Whether your library system has two librarians or 200, some of them probably deserve an award. Just being nominated for an award makes a person feel good, if you believe what the Academy Awards Oscar nominees say.

Nominate deserving librarians every year for local, state, and national awards. (It is a personal rule of mine to nominate as many of our librarians, library clerks, library volunteers, or other of our library affiliated people as I possibly can.) Public recognition for hard-working, effective, talented library workers is well deserved.

There are different ways to decide whom to nominate. One method that has worked successfully is to nominate a librarian at each level every year based on seniority. In order to nominate people without causing hard feelings, develop a process to determine who should be nominated and take that to your library advisory committee. Once the library advisory committee buys into the process, communicate the process to the librarians so that everyone knows the plan. Keep a list of librarians in the school district that shows their hire dates. The first year nominate the elementary, middle and high school librarians who have been in the school district the longest.

Always contact the librarians and ask their permission to nominate them. Once they agree to being nominated, ask them to give you background information about themselves to use in the nomination.

Use what works for you, but using seniority for your first criteria for nominations is practical. For instance, if you have an opportunity to nominate a high school librarian for an award, nominate the most senior of all of your high school librarians. Gather information from the nominee to include in the letter of nomination. Always have the librarian read the nomination letter before sending it so that he can correct any inaccuracies. Provide a copy of the finished nomination to the nominee as well as to his building administrator, the building administrator's supervisor and the director of communications. That way, if the nominee wins the award, no one is surprised and people are well informed by the nomination letter about why the librarian has won the award. See Appendix M for a sample nomination letter.

Keep careful track of the names of the people you have nominated so that each year, you can go to the next most senior person in each category. Be sure to get the nominee's permission before nominating him.

For library volunteers, count on the librarians to provide you with the names of outstanding volunteers. Also, encourage each librarian to nominate volunteers in her library for applicable awards.

There are many library awards that might interest you. Many different organizations offer prizes and awards. Winning a prize or an award can contribute to your district libraries' credibility, give them credentials for seeking grant money, and make the community aware of the positive things that are happening in your libraries. See Figure 9.1 for a chart showing some awards for libraries and librarians.

Figure 9.1

	Awards		
Name of Award	**Sponsoring Organization**	**Amount of Award**	**Program Information**
AASL Collaborative School Library Media Award	Winnebago Software Company and American Association of School Librarians	$2,500	To encourage collaboration between school library media specialists and teachers in meeting the goals in Information Power: Building Partnerships for Learning
AASL Distinguished School Administrators Award	American Association of School Librarians		Outstanding contribution of school librarianship and school library development
Best Practices Award	Boyer Center at Messiah College	$10,000	Family involvement in literacy activities
Grawemeyer Award in Education	University of Louisville	$40,000	Support ideas for improving education
AASL Intellectual Freedom Award	Social Issues Resources Series, Inc.		School library media specialist who has upheld the principles of intellectual freedom
AASL National School Media Program of the Year	Follett Library Resources	$7,000	Excellence and innovation in outstanding library media programs
AASL Information Technology Pathfinder Award	Follett Library Resources		Librarian who demonstrates vision and leadership through the use of information technology
Award for Young Adult Reading or Literature Program	Econo-Clad/YASLA		Development and implementation of an outstanding library program
Grolier Foundation Award	Grolier Foundation		Librarian who makes an unusual contribution to the stimulation and guidance of reading by children and young people
John Cotton Dana Library Public Relations Award	H. W. Wilson Co.		Excellence in public relations programs or special projects
LITA/Gaylord Award	Gaylord Information Systems, Inc.	$1,000	Achievement in library and information technology
Marshall Cavendish Excellence in Library Programming Award	Marshall Cavendish Corporation		Excellence in programming by providing programs that have community impact
National Organization on Disability Award for Library Service for Persons with Disabilities	AETNA US Healthcare		Development of programs or services that make the library's service more accessible through eliminating physical barriers
ALA Goal Award	World Book		Advancement of library service through programs that implement the goals and priorities of ALA
IRA Exemplary Reading Program Award	International Reading Association		Outstanding reading program

continues on next page

Figure 9.1 (continued)

\	Awards		
Name of Award	**Sponsoring Organization**	**Amount of Award**	**Program Information**
William S. Gray Citation of Merit	International Reading Association		Lifetime achievement in the field of reading
Eleanor M. Johnson Award	International Reading Association		Outstanding elementary classroom teacher of reading/language arts
Arbuthnot Award	International Reading Association		Outstanding college teacher of children's and young adult literature
Regie Routman Teacher Recognition Award	International Reading Association		Outstanding teacher who improves teaching through reflective writing
IRA Presidential Award for Reading and Technology	The Learning Company		
ICCONnect ICPrize	American Association of School Librarians		Use of Internet resources to develop meaningful curriculum connections
Webs of Wonder Contest	Analog Science Fiction and Fact and author David Brin	$1,000	Create new Web sites that help colleagues use science fiction in imaginative way in the classroom

There are many contests and awards like this that you can find on the Web. Applying for them is a way to build your writing and marketing skills. Once your school libraries have won one or two awards, the community's perception of your libraries is greatly enhanced.

Advocacy for Libraries and Literacy

Other Public Relations Activities

You might be surprised by how many opportunities there are out there to share positive information about your libraries and librarians. Consider serving on volunteer boards in your community. Networking can present you with golden opportunities to highlight your library staff and programs. Volunteer to be a featured speaker at local retirement centers. Do a book talk, ask for volunteers, and tell them the great things that kids are doing in your libraries. Seize every opportunity to go out into the community to promote your libraries and library workers. Volunteer to speak to local civic organizations and/or write a column for a local newspaper. Create and distribute a monthly library newsletter. These are some of the many ways you can advocate for libraries.

Celebrations

There is nothing like a celebration or special event to put the focus on the library and the library programs. Although a large part of the job is to get the resources to your libraries and librarians and get out of their way so that they can get their jobs done, another part of the job continues to be putting the public focus on your school libraries. Use the following opportunities to highlight libraries and literacy.

Children's Book Week

Elementary librarians can shine a light on their programs by participating in festivities during Children's Book Week. Have librarians in your system share with one another about the activities that they do in their libraries and schools. Sign up to speak on behalf of children's literacy at the school board meeting. Bring librarians dressed as children's book characters to bring smiles to the faces of the board members.

Teen Read Week

Middle and high school librarians can fire up enthusiasm for books and libraries by participating in Teen Read Week. From making their own "Get Caught Reading" posters to making an art video about the school library, students love to participate in this positive library celebration.

Read Across America

Join with the local chapter of the National Education Association (NEA) to pick up the Dr. Seuss theme and "Read Across America" on Dr. Seuss's birthday. There are so many fun activities, from a Dr. Seuss café, to the football team reading to the second graders. Do not miss this chance to salute reading.

National Library Week
The American Library Association (ALA) Web page offers many ideas for celebrating National Library Week. Share these ideas with your librarians and encourage them to share ideas with one another. Make a booklet of ideas the librarians have created and post it on your Web page. Distribute promotional buttons and bookmarks to school board members at the school board meeting.

Working with School and Library Boards
You must develop a positive working relationship with your governing boards. To do this, work together with them over time in a consistently positive, helpful and professional manner. Take an opportunity like Children's Book Week or National Library Week to put a packet of promotional materials in the mail or at the seat of each of your board of education members. Use your themes to make vivid token gifts like student-made plastic plate pocket watches that say it is "Library Time!"

Decorate the board of education meeting room with READ posters. Attend all of the board meetings so that you are familiar with the way your members think and vote. Attend the board meeting during Children's Book Week with the members of your library public relations committee dressed in thematic costumes. Sign up to speak in the open forum to acknowledge the terrific job that your librarians, library staff and volunteers do.

Effective Communication Methods
As the director of a system of libraries, one of your responsibilities is to communicate effectively in order to continuously promote your libraries in a positive and successful manner. There are several tools you can use to do that. The most valuable communication tool you can use is that which has a voice, is persuasive, is easy to read or hear, is non-invasive, and hooks the reader or listener.

Post Library Web Pages
In today's world, every school library needs a well-done library Web page. As library director, you will want a library Web page for your school district or system. You may also want each of your individual libraries to have up-to-date library Web pages. For that to happen, you will need buy-in from all your busy library media specialists.

As you consider designing a Web page, do some research. *Tooting Your Own Horn: Web-Based Public Relations for the 21st Century Librarian* by Julieta Dias Fisher and Ann Hill, published by Linworth Publishing, Inc., is a good resource for both you and for your district librarians when designing library Web pages.

Another good resource for you as you plan your Web page is the Internet itself. Go online and check out other school library Web pages. Compare and contrast them. Share them with all interested parties and see if you can find common areas or features that you want to include in your own Web page.

Give Press Releases

Another way to keep the public informed about your library system and events is with timely press releases. Use press releases when you have good news, a human-interest story, or a special event or celebration. The press release should be short, to-the-point and concise. Include the basic who, what, where, when, and why of journalism. Include the name, phone number, and fax number of the contact person for the story. Be sure that that person knows and approved of you giving the press release before you pull the trigger. Always clear press releases with your supervisor before going public. See Appendix N for a sample press release.

Produce Brochures

Consider developing a brochure to highlight your library system. Do some research and see what other school districts have produced. Explore the attributes of your school library system that you would like to feature. Get help from your communications department, if you have one. Consider working with the career and technical education department to have students help you develop a logo and design the format of the brochure. You can order special brochure paper from many office supply places and print your own brochures on your office printer or you can go out and have the brochure printed in color from a professional. The choice is yours. Be sure to include your addresses and contact numbers. Keep the brochure simple and easy to read. Proofread the document several times before heading to the printer. Figure 9.2, Library Brochure, is one example.

Figure 9.2

Quality Libraries
A quality library is open and staffed by an expert librarian in each school in our district. Our online collection contains more than **one million** (1,000,000) books and related materials.

Our libraries are networked and provide interlibrary loan options in each location. Every school has access to the online catalog which contains entries for our entire collection. Whether our students need print or multimedia materials, we are equipped to meet their needs.

We have a commitment to provide the best of recommended children's and young adult literature and to teach the information management skills necessary for our students to be lifelong readers, learners, and information users.

Summer Libraries
Several of our school libraries are open in the summer to provide quality reading material and innovative programming and instruction to our clients year-round.

Information Management
Students must learn the skills of information management. In our school libraries today, students are preparing to enter the workplace of the 21st century. Students can research topics online; browse electronic journals, encyclopedia, magazines and indexes; and access information from other libraries.

2002-2003 Annual Circulation Averages

	Totals
High School	62,980
Middle School	72,283
Elementary	1,059,307
School Totals District-wide	1,194,570
District Media Centers	7,124
Total	**1,201,694**

Library Staff Committees
Our 55 librarians devote their time and efforts to the task of improving all aspects of the library program.

Several committees meet regularly to make recommendations regarding programs, technology and in-service training.

Library committees are: Author, Cataloging, Multimedia, Gateway, Library Advisory, Library Gift, Professional Development and Public Relations.

Staff and Facilities
Educational assistants and honored volunteers assist our professional librarians in many schools.

Title Library Connections
Title I librarians meet monthly to learn reading strategies that can be implemented during students' library time.

Literature and Skills
The best of children's and young adult literature is available to our students. Librarians foster literacy and the appreciation of good literature. Elementary librarians teach information literacy classes at least once a week to each class.

Per Pupil Expenditures

Avg. per pupil library expenditure in SM in 2001-02	$14.13
Avg. per pupil library expenditure nationally in 2001-02	$16.50
Avg. per pupil library expenditure in SM in 2002-03	$4.37

Average Cost of Library Books 2002-03

Elementary	$20.00
Middle School	$27.00
High School	$35.00

Indian Creek Technology Center, the home of Media Services provides:

- **Central Library Processing** for all library materials

- A **Media Library** of 5,000 video and DVD titles selected to supplement curricula

- A **Professional Library** for the use of Shawnee Mission staff

- **Library Acquisitions** assistance for district librarians with selection resources, budget management, and materials acquisition

- **Instructional Television** programming for classroom teachers and students

- Assistance with **copyright questions** and other staff research needs

---

Shawnee Mission Libraries
Shawnee Mission School District
Shawnee Mission, Kansas

For further information contact:
Cynthia Anderson
Associate Superintendent for Educational Services

Indian Creek Technology Center
4401 West 103rd Street
Shawnee Mission, KS 66207

Phone (913) 993-8701
Facsimile (913) 993-8799
Internet: www.smsd.org
E-mail: cyndeeanderson@smsd.org

Shawnee Mission

Libraries:

Where Learning

is a

Tradition

Publish Electronic Newsletters

This is a simple way to communicate on a regular schedule with your constituents. Publish a monthly online newsletter from you to your library staffs and their supervisors during the school months. The format is easy to set up and easy to deliver once you have developed a distribution list in your email and established a place to post it on your Web page. This newsletter provides an opportunity to communicate with your team, provide information, and build community. Determine which monthly columns you will want to offer in your newsletter. Some suggestions are:

- Celebrations—News items, both personal and professional, are a great way to ensure readership of your newsletter. For example, mention who has a new baby or received a new grant.
- Resources—Relay any free resources that might be available in the community such as free books, willing speakers, or storytellers.
- Opportunities—Staff development opportunities, lectures at local libraries, summer classes for staff, and exchange programs for students and staff can be noted.
- Contests—Include all timely contests that staff or students might enter such as essay contests or National History Day video contest.
- Awards and Honors—Pass along application and contact information on any awards or honors that staff or students might want to apply for.
- Grants—Include information about all grants that might be available for your libraries. No matter how small, winning a grant is a very beneficial thing for your libraries.

Pass along information for both students and staff. Since the newsletter is electronic the recipient can cut and paste and pass along bits of information to their patrons. Read several journals each month and photocopy blurbs of information from them that you might want to relay in your newsletter. Remember to always cite your source of information in case the reader wants more information from the source. There are staff development opportunities as well as grant information in many different journals. Decide how often you will publish, how long your newsletter will be, and what format or layout you will use.

Part of the job of district administrator is to match the opportunities and resources that are out there to the people who might benefit from them. Scouring the journals and Web sites for these and passing the information along is a way to make slim budgets go further and help people feel connected while getting positive publicity for school library people and programs.

Make Presentations

Another way to serve the profession and promote school libraries is to apply and present at local, regional, and national conferences. Do not be shy. Get involved in your local and state library organizations and serve where you are needed. If you have an area of expertise that you could share with others, do so by making a presentation at a professional conference.

Once you have developed a multimedia presentation on a topic, you will have it ready to present in several different venues. For example, you might present a multimedia presentation to encourage family literacy at a school board meeting, at an administrators' meeting, at a parent teacher organization meeting, or at your academic fraternity meeting. Once you have done the work, get out there and share it with others. When planning your presentations, remember to:

- Identify your key points
- Condense your message
- Illustrate the points with clear examples
- Use your best technology
- Make it interesting
- Cite your sources
- Have plenty of handouts or a Web site where the audience can get the handouts

Sometimes, the presentation opportunity is more informal. You may be asked to present on a library/literacy topic to a parent teacher organization, the school board members, the local government officials, state or federal legislators, representatives of higher education, local foundation boards, and civic groups. You should feel ready to accept an invitation to represent and be an advocate for libraries whenever and wherever you are asked.

Do not forget your local, in-house constituents—the teachers and administrators in your own school district. The genuine, enduring support of your administrators and teachers is absolutely critical to the good health and vitality of your library system. Those people need to be fired-up, flag waving library advocates and part of your job is to fire them up.

Publish Articles

Why not take some of those presentations and write them in article form? Submit them for publication. Publishing the good news about your libraries is another way you can build support for your programs. When you are published, it is good for your school district and good for your libraries. There are many opportunities to publish:

- Local or state library organization newsletters
- National library organization journals
- Library journals
- Online journals
- Local newspapers

In addition to publishing yourself, encourage your librarians to publish. That is a very viable way for professional school librarians to contribute to the profession. Encourage librarians to volunteer to review books for journals such as Linworth's *LIBRARY MEDIA CONNECTION* .

Once published, send copies of the published pieces to the principal, superintendent, and others as this provides a good method for making libraries visible.

Make Public Service Announcements

Have you heard those short, thirty- or sixty-second promotions on the radio that are for not-for-profit organizations or causes? How about making one or two on family literacy for your local radio station? ALA, for example, offers short public service announcements promoting reading, libraries and family literacy that you may broadcast on your local educational TV channel. Call the local radio stations and see if you or your librarians can make literacy public service announcements. Your well-written, persuasive announcement just might make prime time. It is a chance for you to tell the community about new services, resources, or special events.

Promote Libraries on TV

TV stations are always looking for good stories. When your high school football players are in the elementary school reading Dr. Seuss books to the children, your TV station might like to film that for the evening news. There are many things that happen in our libraries that the TV producers would like featured. Develop a simple form to use as a press release and require librarians to use the press release to let you know the noteworthy things that are going on in their libraries. Do not forget to share the press release with the district communications person, if you have one, and also with your supervisor.

If your district has access to the local cable educational channel, you may be able to develop library advocacy programming for that station. Programming is usually available for purchase.

Film an Author Teleconference

If you have the capacity, next time you invite a visiting author to your district, feature the author in a live town hall format teleconference. Planning ahead for this opportunity makes great TV programming. Get written permission from the author for taping rights and the rights to rebroadcast the teleconference indefinitely. This gives your librarians the opportunity to show the author tape to each class who has an interest in that author. In addition to being beneficial to students, broadcasting this type of programming can be well-received in your community.

Join and Participate in Professional Organizations

Many of us chose the field of library science and education because we are called to serve. One very important way we can serve our profession is by joining and participating in professional organizations. The American Library Association, the American Association of School Librarians, the International Library Association, and the International Reading Association are just a few of the organizations that promote libraries and reading. Those organizations also have state and local branches that would benefit from your membership. Encourage the librarians to join and participate in these professional organizations. Host regional conferences in your district and volunteer to serve on the local arrangements committee when national conferences come to your community.

Copyright Policy

Copyright Compliance

It is the intent of the Board of Education to adhere to the provisions of the U.S. copyright laws. Unauthorized reproduction and/or use of copyrighted materials is illegal and unethical. Violation of the copyright laws may result in criminal or civil suits and/or appropriate disciplinary action by the school district.

appendix b

Disposal of Materials Procedure

Criteria	Procedure/Steps in Disposing of Material
A. Damaged Material 1. Pages missing 2. Discoloration of material 3. Cover missing 4. Sections damaged beyond repair 5. Water, mold or fire damage 6. Missing sections that cannot be replaced	**A. Damaged Material** 1. Charge student for damaged material if appropriate. 2. Box and label materials as "damaged." 3. Write requisition for warehouse pick-up and disposal. 4. Using the bar code, delete the item from the district database.
B. Obsolete Material Use two of the following items in making your decision. 1. Copyright date of materials more than ten years old. Exceptions should be made for material that is of historical nature, still current or relevant, or material unaffected by time. 2. Inaccurate information 3. Incomplete information 4. Dated information/concepts 5. Illustrations dated or misleading 6. Instructional strategies dated or inappropriate 7. Material with unsuitable treatment of subject matter 8. Stereotyping of race, culture or gender	**B. Obsolete Material** 1. Mark through the school's identification marking on the title page of each obsolete item with a permanent marker. Other identification markings such as on the edges of library material should be obscured so that this material is not mistakenly returned to the school at a later date. 2. Material should be boxed and labeled as "Obsolete Material." 3. Write requisitions and send to warehouse for resale or disposal. 4. Using the bar code, delete the item from the district database.
C. Surplus Material 1. Duplicate or excess number of copies of same material 2. Material from a course no longer being taught in the school 3. Overstocked items 4. No longer meets an instructional need in the school 5. Outlived instructional usefulness 6. Material given as a gift to the school 7. Publisher's samples 8. Material inappropriate for grade levels in the school	**C. Surplus Material** 1. Mark out identification stamps. 2. All school markings should be obscured so that the material is not mistakenly returned to the school at a later date. 3. Material should be boxed and labeled as "surplus material." 4. Write a requisition to have materials sent to warehouse for resale or disposal. 5. Using the bar code, delete the item from the district database.

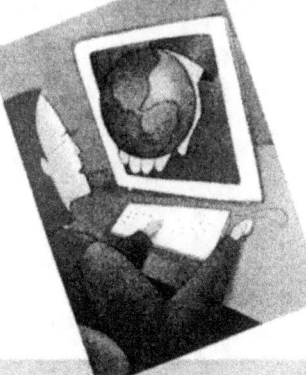

appendix C

Goal Chart

Task	Person	Month											
		Aug	Sept	Oct	Nov	Dec	Jan	Feb	Mar	Apr	May	June	July
1.													
2.													
3.													
4.													
5.													
6.													
7.													
8.													
9.													
10.													

Notes and explanations:

Friends of Libraries

Many people have asked how they could help school libraries during this time of budget cuts. We would love your help and support. There are many ways we could accept help.

Volunteer Time
We need help:
- Shelving library books
- Helping children find books
- Checking books in and out to children and staff
- Checking in new materials, magazines
- Helping at the circulation desk when the librarian is teaching class
- Reading to children
- Labeling special collections

Donations
There are many ways to make donations to your school library.
- Donate your current issues of magazines that the librarian has on her wish list.
- Donate a book in honor of a birthday, a friend, or just because.
- Your librarian will provide you a list of titles s/he would like to receive.
- Donate funds for the librarian to use to select books for purchase.
- (Ask your librarian for a wish list of needed materials to be sure they are appropriate for the collection.)

Bindings of Books
Most often we purchase library books from educational vendors who bind them in a very specialized manner that allows us to get many years of use from a book. While buying us books through the mail or at the bookstore is a very thoughtful act, the shelf life of the book is many years shorter than the bindings that we typically purchase. If you would allow us to purchase from our vendors, you would be ensuring many more circulations of the book.

Book Fairs
If you hold book fairs and wish to donate books or funding to the school library, we would deeply appreciate it. If possible, please allow the librarian to select the books you donate.

Fundraisers

If you wish to hold fund raisers such as bake sales or car washes and donate the proceeds to the school library, we would be honored.

Donations to the School District

Donations of more than $200 must be reported to the Board of Education. The principal at your building can help you initiate that process. Donations of less than $200 do not have to be presented to the Board of Education. Gifts from PTAs are exempt from this procedure. When making a donation to the library fund, please designate that the funds are for library materials. This way the school can deposit the funds in a special 601 account the librarian can use to purchase books.

Lobby Your Legislator

Be sure and contact your legislator to express your opinion about funding a strong public education program in our state.

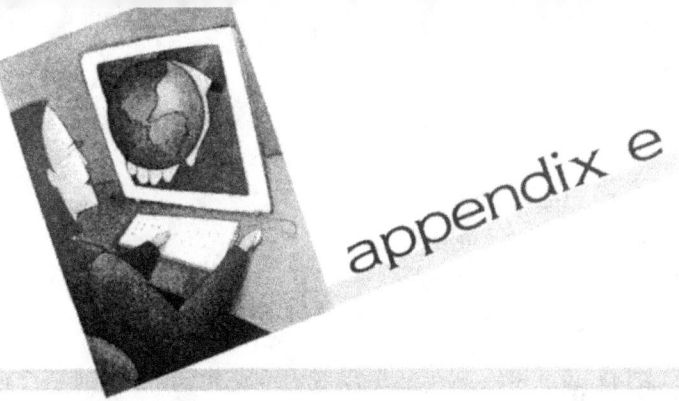

Architectural Requests

Library components should include:

Main Reading Room
- space for two classes (elementary) capable of seating 25-28 students each
- space for three classes (secondary)
- story area (elementary)
- leisure reading area

Library Workroom/Office

Periodical Storage Room (secondary)

Head-end Tech Room

AV Storage Room

Multimedia Editing Bay (secondary)

Conference Room/Professional Library (secondary)

Within the main reading room please include:

Circulation Desk
- Order the circulation desk as part of the library furniture
- Do not custom design it
- Standard height for high school is 39"
- Standard height for elementary is 32"
- Casework adjacent to the circulation desk
- Counter height behind the circulation desk is 39"
- ADA requirements

Story Area
- Area of floor space without tables and chairs
- Available for a story area for young children
- Carpet could have a circle design in that area
- Rocking chair will provide seating for the librarian in that area

Conference Room/Professional Library
- The conference room could also serve as the professional library
- Place a built-in work counter 29" along one wall
- Provide two keyhole workstations
- Provide two computer drops on that counter
- Provide a phone and a data/Internet drop

Library Workroom/Office
- Include a sink in the counter of the workroom
- Include glass windows for supervision
- Standing counter height in the workroom/office is 36"

Further Considerations:

Supervision
Put glass windows 39" from the floor in the
- Office area
- Conference room
- Editing bay

Shelving
- Determine number of volumes to be shelved
- Design for a maximum use of the perimeter walls for bookshelves
- Ideal shelving will be 84" high
- Accommodate light switches, thermostats, and alarms
- Keep island shelving low

Telecommunications
Phones
- Phone jacks in the conference room
- Circulation desk
- Librarian's workroom

Fax
- Fax outlet on the circulation desk
- On the counter in the workroom/office area.

Videoconferencing
Accommodations should be made in the conference room for videoconferencing equipment. A computer data drop, a phone line, and a power source will accommodate.

Computer Technology
   Computer and printer drops
      Consider:
      2 at the circulation desk
      5 at a central large computer station
      4 at the single stand-up stations, spaced throughout the library
      1 in the conference room
      1 in each edit bay
      2 in the head-end tech room
      1 in the workroom/office
      1 in each classroom area

Projection Screens
- Include a projection screen for each classroom
- Automatic electronic control preferred

PA Outlets
   Provide PA outlets in:
- Conference rooms
- Wall behind the circulation desk
- In the workroom
- In the periodical room
- In the head-end tech room

Intercom
   Provide intercom access to:
- Office in the library
- Library workroom/office
- Conference room
- Head-end tech room
- Periodical room
- Editing bay

Clocks
   Provide clocks visible from:
- The checkout desk
- The workroom
- Each of the conference rooms
- The head-end tech room
- The reading room

Cable TV
   Place a cable TV outlet in:
- The classroom areas
- The head-end tech room
- The workroom

Security System
- Design the entrance to the library so that it can accommodate a library security system
- Provide a power source nearby
- Provide an entrance that could handle in/out swinging bars

Location within the School

Locate the library near an outside entrance to the school. The library should be available for evening use without providing public access to the rest of the building. Locate the library adjacent to the building computer lab.

Carpeting

Carpet the library. Please design the carpet so that the area of the reading room that exclusively houses library shelving has its own carpet under it. A border around that area of the main library carpeting would allow re-carpeting the main library in future years without having to re-carpet under the library stacks where less wear occurs.

Lighting
- Provide good lighting for the bookshelves
- Lighting should run parallel to the shelving
- Place task lighting over the circulation desk
- Provide zoned lighting controls in the classroom area. The other areas can remain lighted if the light controls are zoned
- Caution on clerestory lighting and/or skylights
- The computer screens need to be away from bright sunlight

Water and Restrooms
- Place a drinking fountain and restrooms near the library

appendix f

Sample Furniture Specifications

Wooden Wall Shelving
- Avoid hole and peg shelf supports
- Solid oak works best

End Panels
- Exposed vertical edges and bottoms sanded with all corners slightly rounded
- 5/8" grooves for flush mounting aluminum shelf standards
- Recessed shelf standards permit shelf adjustment of 1/2" increments
- Metal clips to be included

Intermediate Upright
- 1" thick solid oak, in height and depth as required
- Exposed vertical edges and bottoms sanded with all corners slightly rounded
- Neither 3/4" nor veneer uprights are acceptable

Cornice (top) Unit
- Cornice panel 3/4" - 13/16" thick solid oak.
- 1 1/4" continuous top w/plastic and backer w/solid oak external bullnose edge bands

Wooden Continuous Top Shelving - Oak
- 2" deep dovetailed top frame
- Countersunk holes for screwing down a continuous top made of high pressure laminate on solid oak
- 3/4" matching edge bands on exposed edges
- Canopy top, flush with uprights acceptable

Tops
- 39", 42", 48" and 60" shelving will have plastic laminate counter tops.

Base
- 3/4" - 13/16" thick by 4" high solid oak kick plate
- Two 3/4" - 13/16" thick 4" wide solid oak bolting blocks

Base Shelf
- 3/4" - 13/16" thick solid oak
- Plywood shelves with veneer are not acceptable

Adjustable shelves
- 3/4" - 13/16" thick solid oak
- Notched at the ends to fit over shelf clips to prevent accidental removal
- Plywood shelves with veneer are not acceptable

Backs
- Oak back panels on all single faced shelving units of oak plywood construction with solid oak framing
- Oak panel dividers for all double faced shelving
- All shelving, both single and double faced, shall have oak panel dividers

Shelving
- Solid oak is best
- 1" thick uprights, 3/4" - 13/16" thick solid oak shelves
- Wood canopy top with 2" solid oak fascia, 1/4" oak plywood back panel and solid oak framing
- All exposed edges banded with solid oak apron

Picture Book
- Wooden dividers, no metal dividers
- Shelves should be 12" deep single faced
- Shelves should be 24" deep double faced

Magazine Shelving
- Stop rail secured to the front of the shelf
- Slanted shelves hinged with adjustable scissor hinge

Tables

1 1/4" thick 5-ply solid lumber core tops with high pressure plastic laminate (hpl) on 5-ply hardwood lumber core work surface. External 1-3/4" or 1-3/8" solid oak bullnose 3/4" radius edge bands applied after top and bottom laminate sheets are applied.

- Solid oak legs are attached with square steel plate
- Particle board tops are not acceptable

Circulation Desk
- 3/4" thick, oak hardwood with oak veneer facing and solid oak edges
- Continuous hpl top over solid oak with external bullnose edge
- Matched for color and grain uniformity and with a solid oak edge
- Particle board tops are not acceptable
- Framing materials kiln-dried hard-wood minimum of 3/4" thick
- Vinyl base mounding 4" high on bases of all circulation desk units
- Computer unit with pullout keyboard tray and grommet hole
- U.L. approved grommets provided for wiring

Depressible Book Truck
- 3/4" oak sides and bottom
- Matching hardwood edge banding
- Four 3"- 4" diameter casters
- Floating shelf surface covered with plastic laminate
- Supported by a spring action depressing mechanism

Book Trucks
- Wooden
- Metal
- Slant-shelf

Lounge Furniture
- Solid oak frames
- Sled base
- Color to match other library furniture
- Interweave fabric

Chairs
- Plain selected red oak
- Straight grain
- Stock free from knots, checks, or other defects affecting durability or appearance

Finish
- Stained to selected finish
- Two coats of sealer
- Two coats of best grade lacquer
- All parts sanded between coats

Construction
- Joints of the rails and back made with mortise and tenon
- Securely glued and multiple doweled
- Seat constructed of solid 1" oak lumber
- Deeply saddled
- Box frame underneath the seat reinforced at all four corners by heavy wood blocks

- Glued and screwed in place
- Back posts bent to put the back at an angle
- Back posts are attached to the side rails by means of mortise and tenon and glue
- Back post is attached to the side rail using a steel bolt and barrel nut

Upholstery
- Top grade

Ergonomic Task Stools
- Swiveled
- Upholstered
- Pneumatic height adjustment
- Adjustable back depth and height
- Height adjustable seat
- Footrest
- Casters

Atlas Stand
- Solid oak all exposed edges banded
- 5 pull-out shelves with stops
- Sloping top with retainer lip

Dictionary Stand
- 24" wide x 42" high x 16" deep sloped top
- Constructed of 3/4" thick seven ply veneer core red oak plywood
- Supported with four vertical solid red oak legs

Newspaper Display
- Compact A frame construction with 10 rods
- 62" high x 32" wide x 19" deep
- Solid oak sides

Podium
- Height manually adjusts from 42" to 52"
- Illuminated reading surface
- Microphone with on/off switch and 6-foot cable
- Volume control
- Four full-range speakers
- 35 watts power output
- Concealed casters
- Oak laminate
- Shelf on backside

Paperback Book Tower
- Frame of solid oak hardwood
- Revolving acrylic towers
- Five tier towers

Desk
- Top of five-ply with lumber core material with bullnosed edge
- One or two pedestal
- Locking drawer

Display Case
- Adjustable shelves
- Light fixture
- Adjustable levelers
- Doors, shelves and tops of clear, tempered safety glass
- Plain white back, or plaque back with a washable Velcro™ surface

Kick Stools
- Steel with plastic base bumper
- Concealed retractable casters
- Rubber safety treads on platform and top
- Support up to 350 lbs.

DEVIATION SHEET

Any deviation from the specifications must be listed below and included with your bid. Failure to do so will cause your bid to be considered as non-responsive.

SPECIFICATIONS ITEM   **BIDDING IN LIEU OF SPECIFIED**

List libraries of similar size bidder has furnished within the last five years:

appendix g

Linking Literature

Linking Literature to Text Structure Activities
Sarah Shaw and Christine Walker
<<sshawrp@mail.olathe.k12.ks.us>> or <<cwalkerac@mail.olathe.k12.ks.us>>
Reprinted with permission from the Olathe School District

Prediction

Character Chart
1. *That Pesky Rat* – Child
2. *The Feet in the Gym* – Daniels
3. *The Recess Queen* – O'Neill
4. *The Ant Bully* – Nickle
5. *New York's Bravest* – Osborne
6. *Snowmen at Night* – Buehner

Prediction Word Bank
1. *The Wolf Who Cried Boy* – Hartman
2. *Rosie's Roses* – Duncan Edwards
3. *Dear Mrs. LaRue: Letters from Obedience School* – Teague
4. *Arnie the Doughnut* – Keller
5. *Old Cricket* – Wheeler
6. *Sorry* – Van Leeuwen

KWL
1. *Supermarket* – Krull
2. *My Soccer Book* – Gibbons
3. *Dinosaur Bones* – Barner
4. *Waiting for Wings* – Ehlert
5. *Chickens May Not Cross the Road and Other Crazy (But True) Laws* – Linz
6. *All You Need for a Snowman* – Schertle

Retelling

Goal Structure Map
1. *Farmer McPeepers and his Missing Milk cows* – Duffield
2. *Muncha, Muncha, Muncha* – Fleming
3. *Do Like a Duck Does* – Hindley
4. *Dirty Little Boy* – Brown
5. *Bedhead* – Palatini
6. *Bringing Down the Moon* – Emmett

Story Element Map
1. *Just Ducky* – Mallat
2. *The Smushy Bus* – Helakoski
3. *My Friend Rabbit* – Rohmann
4. *Porcupining: A Prickly Love Story* – Wheeler
5. *Close Your Eyes* – Banks
6. *Queenie Farmer Had Fifteen Daughters* – Campbell

Circular Story Map
1. *If You Take a Mouse to the Movies* – Numeroff
2. *Pumpkin Jack* – Humbell
3. *If You Take a Mouse to School* – Numeroff
4. *We're Going on a Lion Hunt* – Axtell
5. *This is the Rain* – Schaefer
6. *This is the Sunflower* – Schaefer

Sequence
1. *Scarecrow's Hat* – Brown
2. *Henry Builds a Cabin* – Johnson
3. *One Rainy Day* – Gorbachev
4. *The Magic Hat* – Fox
5. *The House that Jack Built* – Taback

Compare and Contrast

T-Table
1. *Leaving Home* – Collard (Animals/Movement)
2. *Two Little Trains* – Brown (Real/Imaginary)
3. *Hello, Hello* – Schlein (Animal/Greeting)
4. *Snow* – Stojic (Winter/Summer)
5. *Hondo and Fabian* – McCarty (Days activities)
6. *Why do Kittens Purr?* – Bauer (Animal action/Why they do it)

Venn Diagram
1. *Three Pigs* – Wiesner / *Wait! No Paint!* – Whalley
2. *Oliver Finds His Way* – Root / *Quack, Daisy, Quack* – Simmons
3. *Sometimes I'm Bombaloo* – Vail / *When Sophie Gets Really Angry* – Bang
4. *Princess and the Pizza* – Auch / *Princess and the Pea* – Vaes
5. *Joe Cinders* – Mitchell / *Cindy Ellen: A Wild Western Cinderella* – Lowell
6. *Earthquack* – Palatini / *Henny Penny* – Wattenberg

Comprehension

QAR
1. *Roller Coaster* – Frazee
2. *The Name Jar* – Choi
3. *A Fine, Fine School* – Creech
4. *The Teddy Bear* – McPhail
5. *Aunt Claire's Yellow Beehive Hair* – Blumenthal
6. *Freedom Summer* - Wiles

appendix h

Instruction to Support Curricular Objectives

LIBRARY MEDIA CENTER								
INSTRUCTION TO SUPPORT CURRICULAR OBJECTIVES - ENGLISH								
GR	TEACHER	# Cls.	CODE	STATEMENT	UNIT	ASSIGNMENT	DATE	LIBRARIAN SUMMARY
9	Clayton	2	1082.47	Expand information gathering skills.	Library Jeopardy	Learning Center students will view the PowerPoint on library resources. Then they will review what they learned through Jeopardy game.	Oct-03	Created two PowerPoints; one to demonstrate library resources and a Jeopardy game to review what they had learned. Treats for correct answers.
10	Roberts	4	1140.12	Develop personal standards for evaluating and appreciating literature.	Select outside reading book.	Students will select a biography for outside reading.	Oct-03	Booktalked selected biographies.

Appendix H: Instruction to Support Curricular Objectives 139

Indian Creek Brochure

Media Services encompasses Library Technical Services, Instructional Television, Professional/Video Library, and Television production and broadcast.

Instructional Television
- Broadcasts instructional TV programming daily on cable channels 2 and 18
- Provides video duplication services

Library Technical Services
- Catalogs, processes, and ships to schools all library materials
- Supports 1 million item Gateway database
- Provides management and electronic inventory support to librarians

Video and Professional Library
- Offers district staff videos, books, and journals to support SM curriculum
- Serves as resource for research and copyright questions

Special Education
Administrative offices for special education staff and special education records are located at Indian Creek Technology Center. Administrative staff assure compliance with federal and state mandates for services to students with special needs.

Indian Creek Technology Center

Across the Shawnee Mission district 800 certified and classified special education staff members serve 5,000 students with special needs and are committed to providing appropriate services and supports to students with disabilities and those who are gifted.

TV Production/Studio
- Produces award winning videos
- Produces and broadcasts original educational television programming

Information Services
- Provides technical support for the district's voice, video, and data systems
- Repairs electronic equipment
- Maintains and upgrades data networks, telephone systems, and two-channel cable TV network

The Help Desk, as the name suggests, provides a single point of contact for technology work requests.

Curriculum and Instruction
The C & I staff promote quality content and classroom instruction in the areas of language arts, mathematics, science, social studies, and international language.

English as a Second Language staff members facilitate services for district students who are English language learners.

Fine Arts
The performing arts and visual arts resource specialists, the music library, and the art resource library are located at Indian Creek Technology Center.

Resource Center:
- Maintains resource materials in all curricular areas for teacher check-out

Resource Specialists:
- Develop course objectives
- Create curriculum guides
- Plan textbook adoptions
- Create online resources
- Organize the Research & Development Forum
- Develop materials to support curriculum
- Provide teaching strategies and management techniques
- Organize preparatory materials for district and state assessments

Staff Development supports instruction in the district by:
- Developing and delivering professional growth opportunities for all staff
- Providing training for both building and individual inservice opportunities
- Providing year-round technology support and training
- Placing more than 100 student teachers each semester
- Monitoring teachers' individual development plans

Testing Office:
- Distributes testing materials for state and local assessments and processes answer sheets
- Analyzes test results and prepares reports
- Provides data to support buildings' school improvement plans

Career and Technical Education (CTE) staff coordinate all SM business education, family and consumer science, and industrial technology programs in secondary schools and Broadmoor Technical Center. In cooperation with teachers and community connections, CTE provides state-approved, competency-based programs to help prepare high school students for postsecondary education and/or entry-level employment.

Indian Creek Technology Center serves as a support unit for Shawnee Mission district staff. The training rooms and technology labs are used for meetings and for district staff development.

Located at Indian Creek are:
Educational Services:
  Career & Technical Education
  Curriculum and Instruction
    English as a Second Language
    Fine Arts
    Resource Center
    Staff Development
    Testing Offices

Media Services
  Instructional Television
  Library Technical Services
  Video and Professional Libraries
  Special Education
  TV Production/Studio

Information Services
  AV Repair
  Computer Center
  Help Desk

Daycare
Johnson County Parks and Recreation staff provide on-site daycare for children of SMSD employees.

Shawnee Mission Public Schools
Education Division
Cynthia Anderson, Associate Superintendent
Educational Services
www.smsd.org
Indian Creek

IC

Indian Creek Technology Center
4401 W. 103rd Street
Overland Park, KS 66207

Information Services

Educational Services

Career & Technical Ed.

Curriculum & Instruction

English as a Second Language

Fine Arts

Media Services

Special Education

Staff Development

TV Production/Studio

---

142 District Library Administration: A Big Picture Approach

appendix j

Results-Based Staff Development Plan

2003 - 2007

Goal: Reading   Building: _____

| Teacher Results:
What do we need to know and be able to do?
Teachers will use a variety of research-based strategies to:
• improve comprehension
• improve vocabulary
• improve fluency | Teacher Indicators:
What evidence will show that strategies are applied?
• long range plans reflect strategies
• daily lesson plans reflect strategies | Student Indicators:
How will the implementation of this plan affect student success?
• State Assessment
• Iowa Test of Basic Skills
• (building-chosen assessment) |

RESULTS BASED STAFF DEVELOPMENT
READING - ELEMENTARY

Staff Development Goals for all Staff	Staff Development Strategies	Timeline	Person(s) Responsible	Resources	Indicators/ Evaluation
Impact Level (Student achievement, student behaviors) Teachers will document that students' knowledge and skills related to reading comprehension have improved.	Collaborative analysis of student and teacher data collected	On-going	All staff members	Student data Time for staff meeting	Staff meeting minutes Summary of analysis of data
	Make instructional adjustments based upon collected data	On-going	All staff members		
	Assess staff awareness of strategies	Annually in May	All staff members	Staff awareness surveys Time for staff meeting	Staff awareness surveys
	Make adjustments to the school improvement plan	Annually in May	Names of school improvement team members	Time for meeting School improvement plan	List of changes in the school improvement plan
	Make adjustments to the results-based staff development plan	Annually in May	Names of school improvement team members	Time for meeting Results-based staff development plan	List of changes in the results-based staff development plan

Appendix J: Results-Based Staff Development Plan 143

appendix k

Elementary Library Media Center Monthly Report

School_____ Enrollment_____

Circle one
      Aug. Sept. Oct. Nov. Dec. Jan. Feb. Mar. Apr. May June

Circulation

Books (library) _____

Books (classroom) _____

Professional materials _____

Magazines _____

DVDs _____

Videocassettes _____

CD-ROMs _____

Tapes/Cassettes _____

Other _____

Activities and Services

Book talks or reviews _____   Planning sessions with teachers _____
Number of hits on library web page _____

Materials Added

Books _____   Other _____

Appendix K: Elementary Library Media Center Monthly Report

appendix l

Secondary Library Media Center Monthly Report

School_____ Enrollment_____

Circle one

Aug.   Sept.   Oct.   Nov.   Dec.   Jan.   Feb.   Mar.   Apr.   May   June

Circulation

Books (library) _____

Books (classroom) _____

Professional materials _____

Magazines _____

DVDs _____

Videocassettes _____

CD-ROMs _____

Tapes/Cassettes _____

Other _____

Activities and Services

Book talks or reviews _____   Planning sessions with teachers _____

Materials Added

Book _____   other _____

appendix m

Sample Nomination Letter

Dear Selection Committee:

I nominate Jane Doe, a middle school librarian in the Blue Ribbon School District, for the State Association of School Librarians President's Award. It is difficult to say in words what an outstanding middle school librarian she is.

Education: Jane Doe graduated from Cedar Crest College in Allentown, Pennsylvania with a BA in History and Elementary Education. She earned a masters degree in library science at Emporia University.

Job History: Jane Doe was a middle school math teacher in New Jersey. When Jane came to our district, she got back to her true love . . . the middle school library! This is her sixth year at Alpha Middle School.

Accomplishments: It is clear to see that Jane's goal is to make her library a user-friendly place where students and staff feel comfortable. She works with faculty and students to help them all become technologically prepared. Step into her library and see the many ways young people and staff are connected. Students surf the net to find the answers they need, they produce brochures, multimedia projects, and video shorts because they have a facilitative, can do, can teach, can coach, champion librarian.

Always upbeat, always cheerful, always helpful, Jane Doe is a dream librarian. She put the media in library media services and service is her middle name. Helping teachers, helping fellow librarians, helping students—when you spot Jane, you see her interacting in positive, constructive, dynamic ways.

She serves on many different committees. Jane can be counted on to plan the professional development, deliver it, and never take any credit for it. She provides leadership for the school district librarians on the library advisory committee. She serves on both the gift book and multimedia committees. She is the one-woman care committee for sixty plus librarians—always there with a homemade card, the perfect gift of hot tea, and a good novel for the sick, or the sad, or the lonely.

Her principal appreciates her, her colleagues respect her, and her students adore her. Jane Doe deserves the President's Award for her outstanding service to her students and colleagues. Please choose Jane Doe.

Sincerely,

appendix n

Sample Press Release

For Immediate Release: Contact Name: Taylor Glouster
Date: Phone number/E-mail:
Happy Days School District
Event: Visiting Author/Illustrator Program

Happy Days School District is hosting world famous visiting author/illustrator Beatrix Potter. Mrs. Potter will be presenting to elementary students in two sessions during the school day and then later will be presenting to students and parents in an evening session. Each presentation will be followed by an autographing session. Beatrix Potter's books will be for sale at each presentation.

Location:	Date:	Time:
Hunka Munka Elementary School	April 1	9:00 – 11:00 A.M.
Two Bad Mice Elementary School	April 1	1:00 - 3:00 P.M.
Jeremy Fisher Elementary School	April 1	7:00 - 9:00 P.M.

Works Consulted

Books

American Association of School Librarians (AASL) and Association for Educational Communications and Technology (AECT). *Information Literacy Standards for Student Learning.* Chicago, IL: American Library Association, 1998.

American Association of School Librarians (AASL) and Association for Educational Communications and Technology (AECT). *Information Power: Building Partnerships for Learning.* Chicago, IL: American Library Association, 1998.

Anderson, Cynthia. *Write Grants, Get Money.* Worthington, OH: Linworth Publishing, Inc., 2002.

Andronik, Catherine M., ed. *School Library Management.* 4th ed. Worthington, OH: Linworth Publishing, Inc., 1998.

Anglo-American Cataloguing Rules. 2nd ed. Chicago, IL: American Library Association, 2002.

Arter, Judith A. and Busick, Kathleen U. *Practice With Student-Involved Classroom Assessment.* Portland, OR: Assessment Training Institute, Inc., 2001.

Avery, Elizabeth Fuseler, Dahlin, Terry, and Carver, Deborah A. *Staff Development: A Practical Guide.* 3rd ed. Chicago, IL: American Library Association, 2001.

Baule, Steven M. *Facilities Planning for School Library Media and Technology Centers.* Worthington, OH: Linworth Publishing, Inc., 1999.

Baule, Steven M. *Technology Planning for Effective Teaching and Learning.* 2nd ed. Worthington, OH: Linworth Publishing, Inc., 2001.

Becker, Beverley C. and Stan, Susan M. *Hit List for Children 2: Frequently Challenged Books.* Chicago, IL: American Library Association, 2002.

Belcastro, Patricia. *Evaluating Library Staff: A Performance Appraisal System.* Chicago, IL: American Library Association, 1998.

Berger, Pam. *Internet for Active Learners: Curriculum-Based Strategies for K-12.* Chicago, IL: American Library Association, 1998.

Braun, Linda W. *Teens.library: Developing Internet Services for*

Young Adults. Chicago, IL: American Library Association, 2002.

Brown, Carol R. *Interior Design for Libraries: Drawing on Function and Appeal.* Chicago, IL: American Library Association, 2002.

Bucher, Katherine Toth. *Information Technology for Schools.* 2nd ed. Worthington, OH: Linworth Publishing, Inc., 1998.

Bush, Gail. *The School Buddy System: The Practice of Collaboration.* Chicago, IL: American Library Association, 2002.

Buzzeo, Toni. *Collaborating to Meet Standards: Teacher/Librarian Partnerships for K-6.* Worthington, OH: Linworth Publishing, Inc., 2002.

Buzzeo, Toni. *Collaborating to Meet Standards: Teacher/Librarian Partnerships for 7-12.* Worthington, OH: Linworth Publishing, 2002.

Canadian Library Association, Chartered Institute of Library and Information Professionals and American Library Association. *Anglo-American Cataloguing Rules.* 2nd ed. Chicago, IL: American Library Association, 2002.

Carson, Kerry David, Carson, Paula Phillips, and Phillips, Joyce Schouest. *The ABCs of Collaborative Change: The Manger's Guide to Library Renewal.* Chicago, IL: American Library Association, 1997.

Cianciolo, Patricia J. *Informational Picture Books for Children.* Chicago, IL: American Library Association, 2000.

Collins, Jim. *Good to Great: Why Some Conpanies Make the Leap...And Others Don't.* New York: Harper Collins, 2001.

Crews, Kenneth D. *Copyright Essentials for Librarians and Educators.* Chicago, IL: American Library Association, 2000.

Derrick, Thomas E. *District Centralized Processing for School Library Media Centers: Theories, Integration, and Utilization.* 1998.

Doll, Carol A. and Barron, Pamela Petrick. *Managing and Analyzing Your Collection: A Practical Guide for Small Libraries and School Media Centers.* ALA Editions, 2002.

Driggers, Preston and Dumas, Eileen. *Managing Library Volunteers: A Practical Toolkit.* Chicago, IL: American Library Association, 2002.

Eisenberg, Michael B. and Berkowitz, Robert E. with Jansen, Barbara A. and Little, Tami J. *Teaching Information & Technology Skills: The Big6™ in Elementary Schools.* Worthington, OH: Linworth Publishing, Inc., 1999.

Eisenberg, Michael B. and Berkowitz, Robert E. with Darrow,

Robert, and Spitzer, Kathleen. *Teaching Information & Technology Skills: The Big6™ in Secondary Schools.* Worthington, OH: Linworth Publishing, Inc., 2000.

Eisenberg, Michael B. and Berkowitz, Robert E. *The Big6™ Collection: The Best of the Big6 Newsletter.* Worthington, OH: Linworth Publishing, Inc., 2000.

Erikson, Rolf and Markuson, Carolyn. *Designing a School Library Media Center for the Future.* American Association of School Librarians, 2001.

Everhart, Nancy. *Evaluating The School Library Media Center.* Englewood, CO: Libraries Unlimited, Inc., 1998.

Facilities Guidelines for Library Media Programs. Baltimore, MD: State Department of Education, 1998.

Farmer, Lesley S. J. *Partnerships for Lifelong Learning.* 2nd ed. Worthington, OH: Linworth Publishing, Inc., 1999.

Feinberg, Sandra, Kuchner, Joan F., and Feldman, Sari. *Learning Environments for Young Children: Rethinking Library Spaces and Services.* Chicago, IL: American Library Association, 1998.

Fisher, Julieta Dias and Hill, Ann. *Tooting Your Own Horn: Web-Based Public Relations for the 21st Century Librarian.* Worthington, OH: Linworth Publishing, Inc., 2002.

Flowers, Helen F. *Public Relations for School Library Media Programs: 500 Ways to Influence People and Win Friends for Your School Library Media Center.* New York: Neal-Schuman Publishers, 1998.

Giesecke, Joan. *Practical Strategies for Library Managers.* Chicago, IL: American Library Association, 2001.

Glandon, Shan. *Integrating Technology: Effective Tools for Collaboration.* Worthington, OH: Linworth Publishing, Inc., 2002.

Hafner, Arthur W. *Descriptive Statistical Techniques for Librarians.* 2nd ed. Chicago, IL: American Library Association, 1998.

Hartzell, Gary. *Building Influence for the School Librarian: Tenets, Targets, & Tactics, Second Edition.* Worthington, OH: Linworth Publishing, Inc., 2003.

Hopkins, Janet. *Assistive Technology: An Introductory Guide for K-12 Library Media Specialists.* Worthington, OH: Linworth Publishing, Inc., 2004.

Intellectual Freedom Manual. Chicago, IL: American Library Association, 2002.

Johnson, Doug. *The Indispensable Librarian: Surviving (and Thriving) in School Media Centers in the Information Age.* Worthington, OH: Linworth Publishing, Inc., 1997.

Johnson, Doug. *The Indispensable Teacher's Guide to Computer Skills.* 2nd ed. Worthington, OH: Linworth Publishing, Inc., 2002.

Kahn, Miriam B. *Disaster Response and Planning for Libraries.* 2nd ed. Chicago, IL: American Library Association, 2002.

Kan, Katharine L. *Sizzling Summer Reading Programs for Young Adults.* Chicago, IL: American Library Association, 1998.

Kaplan, Allison G. and Riedling, Ann Marlow. *Catalog It! A Guide to Cataloging School Library Materials.* Worthington, OH: Linworth Publishing, Inc., 2002.

Karolides, Nicholas, ed. *Censored Books II: Critical Viewpoints, 1985-2000.* Lanham, MD: Scarecrow Press, 2002.

Karp, Rashelle S., ed. *Powerful Public Relations A How-To Guide for Libraries.* Chicago, IL: American Library Association, 2002.

Kasowitz, Abby. *Using the Big6™ To Teach and Learn With the Internet.* Worthington, OH: Linworth Publishing, Inc., 2000.

Killion, Joellen. *Assessing Impact: Evaluating Staff Development.* Oxford, OH: National Staff Development Council, 2002.

Kuharets, Olga R. *Venture into Cultures: A Resource Book of Multicultural Materials and Programs.* 2nd ed. Chicago, IL: American Library Association, 2001.

Krashen, Stephen. *The Power of Reading: Insights from the Research.* Englewood, CO: Libraries Unlimited, 1993.

Lance, Keith Curry. *How School Libraries Improve Outcomes for Children: The New Mexico Study.* Castle Rock, CO: Hi Willow Research and Publishing, 2003.

Lance, Keith Curry, Hamilton-Pennell, Christine, and Welborn, Lynda Blackburn. *The Impact of School Library Media Centers on Academic Achievement.* Castle Rock, CO: Hi Willow Research and Publishing, 1997.

Lance, Keith Curry, Rodney, Marcia J., and Hamilton-Pennell, Christine. *Good Schools Have School Librarians: Oregon School Librarians Collaborate to Improve Academic Achievement.* Terrebonne, OR: Oregon Educational Media Association, 2001.

Lance, Keith Curry, Rodney, Marcia J., and Hamiton-Pennell, Christine. *How School Librarians Help Kids Achieve Standards: The Second Colorado Study.* Castle Rock, CO: Hi Willow Research and Publishing, 2000.

Lance, Keith Curry, et al. *Measuring Up to Standards: The Role of School Libraries and Information Literacy.* Denver, CO: Library Research Service, 1999.

Lance, Keith Curry and Loertscher, David V. *Powering Achievement: School Library Media Programs Make a Difference: The Evidence.* 2nd ed. Castle Rock, CO: Hi

Willow Research & Publishing, 2002.

Lesesne, Teri S. and Chance, Rosemary. *Hit List for Young Adults 2: Frequently Challenged Books.* Chicago, IL: American Library Association, 2002.

Loertscher, David V. *Collection Mapping in the LMC: Building Library Media Center Collections in the Age of Technology.* Castle Rock, CO: Hi Willow Research and Publishing, 1996.

Loertscher, David V. *Reinventing Your School's Library in the Age of Technology: A Guide for Principals and Superintendents.* Castle Rock, CO: 2002.

Loertscher, David V. *Taxonomies of the School Library Media Program.* 2nd ed. Hi Willow Research and Publishing, 2000.

Loertscher, David V. and Achterman, Douglas. *Increasing Academic Achievement Through the Library Media Center: A Guide for Teachers.* Castle Rock, CO: Hi Willow Research and Publishing, 2002.

Loertscher, David V. and Woolls, Blanche. *Information Literacy: A Review of the Research.* 2nd ed. Castle Rock, CO: Hi Willow Research and Publishing, 1999.

Loertscher, David V., Woolls, Blanche, and Felker, Janice. *Building a School Library Collection Plan: A Beginning Handbook with Internet Assist.* Castle Rock, CO: Hi Willow Research and Publishing, 1998.

Logan, Debra Kay and Beuselinck, Cynthia Lee. *K-12 Web Pages: Planning & Publishing Excellent School Web Sites.* Worthington, OH: Linworth Publishing, Inc., 2002.

McConnell, Terry and Sprouse, Harry W. *Video Production for School Library Media Specialists: Communication and Production Techniques.* Worthington, OH: Linworth Publishing, Inc., 2000.

McElmeel, Sharron L. *ABC's of an Author/Illustrator Visit.* 2nd ed. Worthington, OH: Linworth Publishing, Inc., 2001.

McKenzie, Jamie. *How Teachers Learn Technology Best.* Worthington, OH: FNO Press, 1999.

McKenzie, Jamie. *Planning Good Change with Technology and Literacy.* Worthington, OH: FNO Press, 2001.

Mason, Marilyn Gell. *Strategic Management for Today's Libraries.* Chicago, IL: American Library Association, 1999.

Mayo, Diane and Nelson, Sandra. *Wired for the Future: Developing Your Library Technology Plan.* Chicago, IL: American Library Association, 1999.

Michie, J., and Chaney, B. *Assessment of the Role of School and Public Libraries in Support of Education at Reform.*

Rockville, MD: Westat, 2000.

Milbury, Peter, Eisenberg, Michael B., and Walker, Michelle. *The Best of LM_NET Select 2001*. Worthington, OH: Linworth Publishing, Inc., 2002.

Miller, Donna. *The Standards-Based Integrated Library: A Collaborative Approach for Aligning the Library Program with the Classroom Curriculum, 2nd Edition*. Worthington, OH: Linworth Publishing, Inc., 2004.

Minkel, Walter and Feldman, Roxanne Hsu. *Delivering Web Reference Services to Young People*. Chicago, IL: American Library Association, 1998.

Nelson, Sandra, Altman, Ellen, and Mayo, Diane. *Managing for Results: Effective Resource Allocation for Public Libraries*. Chicago, IL: American Library Association, 2000.

Nesbeitt, Sarah L. and Gordon, Rachel Singer. *The Information Professional's Guide to Career Development Online*. Medford, NJ: Information Today, 2002.

Pappas, Marjorie L., Geitgey, Gayle A., and Jefferson, Cathy A. *Searching Electronic Resources*. 2nd ed. Worthington, OH: Linworth Publishing, Inc., 1999.

Piepenburg, Scott. *More Easy MARC: Incorporating Format Integration*. 4th ed. Castle Rock, CO: Hi Willow Research and Publishing, 2002.

Piepenburg, Scott. *MARC Authority Records Made Easy: A Simplified Guide to Creating Authority Records for Library Automation System*s. Castle Rock, CO: Hi Willow Research and Publishing, 2000.

Price, Anne and Yaakov, Juliette. *Children's Catalog*. New York, NY: H.W. Wilson, 2001.

Program Evaluation: Library Media Services. Schaumburg, IL: National Study of School Evaluation (NSSE), 1998.

Public Education Network (PEN) and American Association of School Librarians (AASL), Sandra Hughes-Hassell, and Anne Wheelock, eds. *The Information-Powered School*. Chicago, IL: American Library Association, 2001.

Reichman, Henry. *Censorship and Selection: Issues and Answers for Schools*. 3rd ed. Chicago, IL: American Library Association, 2001.

Riedling, Ann Marlow. *Reference Skills for the School Library Media Specialist: Tools and Tips*. Worthington, OH: Linworth Publishing, Inc., 2000.

Sáez, Eileen Elliott de. *Promoting the School Library*. 2nd ed. Swindon, Great Britain: School Library Association, 2000.

Saffady, William. *Introduction to Automation for Librarians*. 4th ed. Chicago, IL: American Library Association, 1999.

Safford, Barbara Ripp and Nichols, Margaret Irby. *Guide to Reference Materials for School Library Media Centers*.

Englewood, CO: Libraries Unlimited, 1998.

Sannwald, William W. *Checklist of Library Building Design Considerations.* 4th ed. Chicago, IL: American Library Association, 2001.

Santa Clara (CA) County Office of Education, Library Services. *Where Do I Start? A School Library Handbook.* Worthington, OH: Linworth Publishing, Inc., 2001.

Scales, Pat R. *Teaching Banned Books: 12 Guides for Young Readers.* Chicago, IL: American Library Association, 2001.

Schrock, Kathleen, editor. *The Technology Connection: Building a Successful School Library Media Program.* Worthington, OH: Linworth Publishing, Inc., 2000.

Shaw, Marie Keen. *Block Scheduling and Its Impact on the School Library Media Center.* Westport, CT: Greenwood Press, 1999.

Shuman, Bruce A. *Library Security and Safety Handbook: Prevention, Policies, and Procedures.* Chicago, IL: American Library Association, 1999.

Simmons, John S. and Dresang, Eliza T. *School Censorship in the 21st Century: A Guide for Teachers and School Library Media Specialists.* Worthington, OH: Linworth Publishing, Inc., 2001.

Simpson, Carol. *Copyright for Schools: A Practical Guide.* 3rd ed. Worthington, OH: Linworth Publishing, Inc., 2001.

Simpson, Carol and McElmeel, Sharron L. *Internet for Schools: A Practical Guide.* 3rd ed. Worthington, OH: Linworth Publishing, Inc., 2000.

Spencer, Gwynne. *Have Talent, Will Travel: Directory of Authors, Illustrators and Storytellers West of the Mississippi.* Worthington, OH: Linworth Publishing, Inc., 2002.

Smith, G. Stevenson. *Accounting for Libraries and Other Not-For-Profit Organizations.* 2nd ed. Chicago, IL: American Library Association, 1999.

Smith, G. Stevenson. *Managerial Accounting for Libraries and Other Not-for-Profit Organizations.* 2nd ed. Chicago, IL: American Library Association, 2002.

Stein, Barbara L. and Brown, Risa W. *Running a School Library Media Center.* 2nd ed. New York, NY: Neal-Schuman Publishers, 2002.

Taney, Kimberly Bolan. *Teen Spaces: The Step-by-Step Library Makeover.* Chicago, IL: American Library Association, 2002.

Valenza, Joyce Kasman. *Power Research Tools: Learning Activities and Posters.* Chicago, IL: American Library Association, 2002.

Valenza, Joyce Kasman. *Power Tools: 100+ Essential Forms and*

Presentations for Your School Library Information Program. Chicago, IL: American Library Association, 1998.

Van Orden, Phyllis. *Selecting Books for the Elementary School Library Media Center: A Complete Guide.* New York: Neal-Schuman Publishers, 2000.

Veccia, Susan H. *Uncovering Our History: Teaching With Primary Sources.* Chicago, IL: American Library Association, 2003.

Wallace, Linda K. *Libraries, Mission, and Marketing: Writing Mission Statements That Work.* Chicago, IL: American Library Association, 2003.

Wasman, Ann M. *New Steps to Service: Common-Sense Advice for the Library Media Specialist.* Chicago, IL: American Library Association, 1998.

Willis, Mark. *Dealing with Difficult People in the Library.* Chicago, IL: American Library Association, 1999.

Wilson, Patricia Potter and Lyders, Josette Anne. *Leadership for Today's School Library: A Handbook for the Library Media Specialist and the School Principal.* Westport, CT: Greenwood Press, 2001.

Wolinsky, Art. *Internet Power Research Using the Big6™ Approach.* Worthington, OH: Linworth Publishing, 2002.

Woodward, Jeannette A. *Countdown to a New Library: Managing the Building Project.* Chicago, IL: American Library Association, 2000.

Woolls, Blanche. *The School Library Media Manager.* 2nd ed. Englewood, CO: Libraries Unlimited, 1999.

Young Adult Library Services Association (YALSA), Mary K. Chelton, ed. *Excellence in Library Services to Young Adults: The Nation's Top Programs*

Video

Eisenberg, Michael B. *Essential Skills for the Information Age: The Big6™ in Action.* Worthington, OH: Linworth Publishing, Inc., 1999.

McColgin, Michael. *Disaster Planning.* Chicago, IL: American Library Association, 2000.

Website

Gordon, Andrew. Public Access Computing Project. University of Washington. <<http://www.gspa.Washington.edu/research/current/html#access>>

Schmidt, William D., Reick, Donald Arthur, Vicek, Carles W. *Managing Media Services Theory and Practice.* <<http://www.netLibrary.com/urlapi.asp?action=summary&v=1&bookid=33388>>

index

21st Century Community Learning Center Grant, 83
3M™, 89, 105

A

Accelerated Reader™, 40
Accessibility, 65
Acoustics, 60, 64
Acquisitions, 37, 38
ADA
    codes, 65
    compliance, 57
    requirements, 61, 65, 71, 125
    standards, 61
Adequate Yearly Progress (AYP), 98
Administration, 78
Administrator
administrators, 13
Advertising, 4
Advocacy, 103, 109
Age discrimination, 5
Air shift desk, 69
American Library Association (ALA), 16, 97, 110, 115, 153, 154, 155, 156, 157, 158, 159, 160, 161
American Association of School Librarian's Highsmith Research Grant, 52
American Association of School Librarians (AASL), 89, 115, 153, 155, 158
Antiquarian Book, 40
Approval
approvals, 51
Assistive Technology – An Introductory Guide, 63, 155
Authors, 22, 159
AV
    AV hardware, 69
    AV repair area, 69
    AV software, 69

B

Banned Books Week, 76
Banners, 4
Barbara Bush Foundation for Family Literacy, 53
Behavioral interviewing, 9
Bibliography, 22, 153
Big book storage and display, 66
Blind or window covering, 56
Board of education, 16
    policy, 16
    policy book, 16
Book
    talks, 79
    trucks, 131
Braille, 61
Broadcasting
Broadcast equipment, 69
Brochure, 112, 141
brochures, 111
Budget, 22, 28, 33, 35, 41, 45
budgeting, 46
    per Pupil, 46, 47

C

Calendar, 21, 76
Cancer, 7
Capital
    budgets, 47
Cappuccino day, 48
Carpet, 56, 126, 128
carpet or flooring replacement, 56
Cataloging, 12, 31, 36, 37, 156
Ceilings, 56
Celebration
celebrations, 109, 113
Censorship, 41, 158, 159
Certification, 10
Circulation, 23, 43, 65, 84, 125, 131
    data, 233
    desk, 65
    statistics, 23
Civil Rights Act, 5
Classroom, 60, 64, 153, 158
Clocks, 59, 127
Collection, 23, 31, 32, 34, 35, 38, 40, 42, 61, 62, 70, 154, 157
    analysis, 34
Committees, 98
Comprehension, 137

Index 161

Conference rooms, 68
Consolidated Omnibus Budget Reconciliation Act, 5
Contests, 105, 113
Copyright, 17, 18, 37, 117, 154, 159
clearinghouse, 37
Copyright for Schools, A Practical Guide, Third Edition, 18
date, 119
CPU, 65
Curriculum, 12, 13, 22, 38, 77, 81, 153, 158

D

Department of Labor, 5
Dewey classification, 24, 34, 35
Digital
video, 69
video playout system, 69
Director, 13, 14, 100
Disabilities, 5
Disaster, 55, 73, 74, 156, 160
Disasters, 73
recovery, 55
Display, 66, 68, 89, 133
Distance learning, 69, 99
Distance learning equipment, 69
District resource centers
district centers, 84
Donations, 123, 124
Drugfree Workplace Act, 5
Durability, 67
Duties and responsibilities, 8
DVD, 66, 96
burners, 66
DVDs, 90, 145, 147
players, 90

E

Educational Technology State Grants, 51
Educational TV, 4
EEOC, 7
Elementary and Secondary Education Act (ESEA), 6, 10, 51
Elementary schools, 90, 154
Employee Polygraph Protection Act, 6
Employees Retirement Insurance Security Act, 6
Employment, 5
English Language Learners (ELL), 82
Entrances, 68
Equal Employment Opportunity Commission, 7
Equal Pay Act, 6
Equipment, 8, 64, 66, 70, 86

E-rate, 85, 87, 88
Evaluation
evaluate, 29, 35
Exemption status, 8

F

Facilities, 55, 153, 155
Fair Labor Standards Act, 6
Fines, 50
Fire, 59, 73, 74
alarms, 59
Floor seating, 66
FLSA, 6
FMLA, 6
Foundations, 50
Funding, 45, 52, 83
fundraisers, 48
fundraising, 48
Furniture, 47, 56, 57, 63, 64, 70, 71, 129, 131
furnishings, 68
furniture and/or shelving replacement, 57

G

Goals, 27, 84, 95
Grant, 50, 51, 52, 53
funds, 50, 52
grants, 53, 84, 113, 153
GrantsAlert, 53
Group health plan, 5
Guidelines, 8, 155

H

Handbook, 20, 21, 24, 157, 159, 160
Hardware requirements, 42
Health Insurance Portability and Accountability Act (HIPAA), 6
High school libraries, 89
Hiring, 3, 4, 5, 12
decisions, 9
Holdings, 33, 34
HVAC, 56

I

ID badge, 11
Immigration Reform and Control Act, 6
Impact Aid, 53
Improving Literacy Through School Libraries, 51
Index, 21
Information Power Building Partnerships for Learning, 84

Installation, 70
Institute for Library and Information Literacy Education (ILILE), 52
Insurance, 73
International Library Association, 115
International Reading Association, 115
International Society for Technology Education (ISTE), 80
Internet
    access, 67, 87, 91
    filtering, 87, 88
    filtering system, 87
Interview, 8
interviewing, 8, 9, 12
Iowa Test of Basic Skills, 21, 78
Iowa Test of Education Development (ITED), 78
ISTE (International Society for Technology in Education), 78, 80
ITV production center, 90

J
Job title, 8

L
Labeling, 70, 123
Laura Bush Foundation for America's Libraries, 52
Lawrence High School Library, 88
Laws, 5, 17, 135
Leadership, 24, 100, 160
Leave, 6, 73
Lectures, 97
Library
    director, 15
    director's or administrator's handbook, 16
Library Bill of Rights, 16, 19
Library Media Connection, 32, 114
Library Services Technology Act (LSTA), 52
    newsletter, 88
    staffing, 13
Licensure, 10
Light switches, 59
Lighting, 59, 60, 67, 69, 128
Long-range plan
    staff development goals, 95
    strategic plan, 25
Loss of computer system, 74
Loss or contamination of data, 74
LSTA, 52

M
Maintenance, 13, 55
Manual, 12, 155
Mold, 73, 74
Movable storage, 66
MUSTIE method, 40

N
National Assessment of Educational Performance (NAEP), 78
National Education Association (NEA), 109
National History Day video contest, 113
National Library Week, 23, 76, 98, 110
National Origin Discrimination Guidelines, 6
National School Board Association, 19
National Staff Development Council, 94, 156
National Study of School Evaluation (NSSE), 84, 158
Networking, 109
Newsletters, 4, 113
No Child Left Behind, 6, 10, 51, 82, 98

O
Objectives, 27, 79, 82, 139
Occupational Safety Health Act, 6
Omnibus Budget Reconciliation Act, 6
Online
    resources, 17
    tutorials, 97
Open checkout, 76
Ordering, 31, 36
Orientation, 11, 12
Out of district travel, 99

P
Paint, 56, 137
painting, 56
Paraprofessional
paraprofessionals, 10
Parent Teacher Associations, 83
PTA, 84, 124
Performance, 7, 153
Periodical, 40, 125, 127
periodicals, 22, 66
Phone, Internet access, data and cable TV drops, 67
Photos, 88
Plagiarism, 77
Policies, 5, 15, 16, 19, 20, 22, 159
policies and procedures, 15
policy, 16, 17, 19, 31, 117

Posting, 4, 7
Power
    outlets, 67
Power of Literacy, 53
Pregnancy, 6
Pregnancy Discrimination Act, 6
Presentation, 64
Presentations, 113, 159
Preview, 98
Principals, 12, 13, 157
Problem-solving, 28
Procedure, 119
procedures, 12, 18, 22, 159
Processing, 31, 36, 37, 154
Production sets, 69
Program Evaluation Library Media Services, 84, 158
Programming, 38, 75, 82, 83, 90, 107
programs, 11, 12, 53, 107, 155, 156, 160
Promotion, 23
Promotional materials, 69
Public address system, 59
Purchasing, 31, 36, 60, 86

R

Read Across America, 23, 109
READ posters, 110
Reading
Reading is Fundamental (RIF), 52
reading/language arts teachers, 22
    table, 66
Recruiting, 4, 7, 12
recruitment, 3
Referrals, 4
Refugee and immigrant families, 82
Regional conferences, 99
Rehabilitation Act of 1973, 6
Religious Discrimination Guidelines, 7
Replacing furniture, 57
Research, 52, 73, 83, 156, 157, 158, 159, 160
Restrooms, 69, 128
Results-based, 143
    staff development, 143
    staff development plan, 143
Rocking chair, 66, 126
Rosters, 21

S

Salary grade and range, 8
Satellite
    links, 69
    tuners, 66
Scheduling, 13, 75, 76, 159
    fixed scheduling, 76
School
    improvement plan, 13, 23
    library media specialist's handbook, 16
SchoolGrants, 53
Screening, 3, 12
Seat height, 63
Security, 66, 68, 69, 83, 89, 128, 159
Selection, 16, 23, 31, 37, 149, 158
Shelving, 56, 57, 59, 61, 62, 63, 67, 70, 123, 126, 130
    picture book shelving, 66
Signs, 4
signage, 61
Smoke damage, 73
Software, 86
Special collections, 88
Special programming, 82
Specifications, 64, 129
Stacks, 59
Staff development, 13, 38, 94, 96, 97, 99, 143, 153, 156
    opportunities, 113
Standards, 6, 80, 83, 84, 89, 153, 154, 156, 158
Stanford Achievement Test (SAT 10), 78
Starbucks Foundation, 53
State law, 7
Statement of Purpose, 26
Statistics, 23
Storage, 65, 66, 69, 70, 125
Strategic planning, 25
Strobes, 59
Student achievement, 84
    scores, 84
Student policy handbooks, 16
Superintendent, 13, 157
Switchers, 69

T

Tables, 63, 130
Tape duplication capacity, 66
Tape storage, 66
Teacher planning time, 9

Teen Read Week, 23, 109
Teleconference, 115
teleconferences, 99
Telephony equipment, 66
Test scores, 21, 28
Texas State Library, 35, 40
The Children's Catalog, 40
The Children's Internet Protection Act (CIPA), 88
Timeline, 72, 95
Title I, 6, 51, 82
Title I-B4, 51
Title II-D, 51
Training, 10, 28, 153
Tutorials and guides, 88
TV
    production studios, 38, 90
    program production, 66
    studio, 66

U

U.S. Department of Education, 51, 53, 63
Universal Service Administrative Company's Schools and Libraries Division, 87

V

VCR, 90
VCR/DVD, 90
VCRs, 90
VHS camera, 90
Video, 62, 66, 90, 141, 157, 160
    distribution system, 66
    juke box playout system, 66
videocassette/DVD, 38
videoconferencing/editing equipment, 67
Virtual tour, 88
Voice and data drops, 66, 67
Volunteers, 104, 154
    volunteer, 4, 123

W

Walls, 56
Water, 69, 73, 74, 119, 128
    water or flood, 74
Weeding, 19, 38, 39, 40, 72
Windows, 60, 67
Wireless labs and laptops, 89
Work schedule, 8
Workroom, 67, 125
Write Grants, Get Money, 51, 84, 153

Index 165

www.ingramcontent.com/pod-product-compliance
Lightning Source LLC
Chambersburg PA
CBHW081154290426
44108CB00018B/2549